The Liberating Pulpit

The Liberating Pulpit

Justo L.
GONZÁLEZ

& Catherine G.
GONZÁLEZ

Abingdon Press
Nashville

THE LIBERATING PULPIT

Copyright 1994 Abingdon Press

Some of the material in this book is derived but thoroughly revised from *Liberation Preaching: The Pulpit and the Oppressed*, 1980.

This book is printed on acid-free recycled paper.

Library of Congress Cataloging-in-Publication Data

González, Justo L.
   The liberating pulpit / Justo L. González and Catherine G. González.
      p. cm.
   Includes bibliographical references and index.
   ISBN 0-687-33844-1 (alk. paper)
   1. Preaching. 2. Liberation theology. 3. Bible—Criticism, interpretation, etc. I. GonzÁlez, Catherine Gunsalus. II. Title.
BV4211.2.G645   1994
251—dc20   93-23500
                                                                              CIP

94 95 96 97 98 99 00 01 02 03—10 9 8 7 6 5 4 3 2 1

MANUFACTURED IN THE UNITED STATES OF AMERICA

To each other,
     again

Contents

Preface

This book is a thorough revision of *Liberation Preaching: The Pulpit and the Oppressed*, which was first published in 1980. At that time, there were many who claimed that liberation theology was a fad that would quickly pass, as had earlier been the case with a number of theological fashions that briefly made headlines, simply to disappear almost as quickly as they had arisen. Also, there were many, even in theological schools, whose only knowledge of liberation theology was what they read in journalistic interpretations. Since most of those interpretations presented liberation theology as little more than a justification for violence and revolution, we felt compelled to correct that view by showing that liberation theology did indeed deal with the traditional themes of Christian theology, albeit from a different perspective. For similar reasons, we also felt the need to show that various views, concerns and perspectives should properly be included under the heading of liberation theology. Finally, and again for the same reasons, we saw the need to include in the first chapter a brief summary of the main traits and tenets which the various liberation theologies held in common.

Now the situation has changed. The bibliography on the various theologies of liberation is vast, and is still growing at an ever faster pace. The persistence and growing vigor of Latin American liberation theology even after the demise of the Soviet Union and international communism has clearly contradicted those who claimed that such theology was merely a tool of communist subversion, or that it was so tied with orthodox Marxism that the fall of one would necessarily mean the disappearance of the other.

For these reasons, we no longer feel the need to provide an introduction nor an apology for liberation theologies, and therefore the sections in the previous volume which dealt with such matters have either been deleted or greatly reduced. Still, we have felt it necessary to state clearly the theological perspective from which this book is written.

In addition, our own developing interests, and the reports we have received from the use of the previous volume, have left their imprint on the present revision.

Already at the time when *Liberation Preaching* was written, there were other interests lurking between the lines. These were interests which both of us had been pursuing for some time, and which have profoundly affected our understanding of preaching and of biblical interpretation, but which were not explicit in that earlier book. For us, they are tied to the central issues of liberation theology, but in ways that then were not clear. In order to clarify the scope of the revisions leading to the present volume, therefore, it is necessary to make those interests explicit, and to make explicit also how they might relate to the task of preaching—more specifically, to the task of preaching for liberation.

We are both historians of doctrine. Justo's own interests lie in the field of patristic theology, particularly second-century theology. Catherine's are more in the field of liturgics and the theological significance of liturgy.

Catherine's interest has been particularly in the liturgies of the second through the fourth centuries, in the sermons that have remained from that period, and in the use of the Bible in worship.[1] There she has found a vision of preaching that she feels must be recaptured. In that context, she is particularly interested in the relationship between sermon and liturgy.

Justo's interest in patristic theology has focused, among other things, on the patristic interpretation of Scripture,[2] and on how this relates to patristic theology in general. He has also done extensive research on what early Christian writers—up to the time of Augustine—had to say on issues such as the origins and proper use of wealth, the rights and duties of the poor and of the rich, the nature of ownership, etc.[3] Obviously, these are all issues which have a direct bearing on the subject of this book. Although there were already indications of these matters in *Liberation Preaching*, the present volume seeks to pursue them more fully.

Also, for several years Justo has been actively involved in the United Methodist Roundtable of Ethnic Minority Theologians, whose yearly meetings have significantly enriched his understanding of several of the liberation theologies mentioned in the pages that follow.[4] Although the previous version sought to take into account, and to give voice to, these different minority perspectives within the church, it is hoped that this new book will provide further insight into such perspectives.

Finally, this revision has also taken into account the reports we have received of the manner in which the earlier book has been used. Such reports tend to highlight two uses. First, *Liberation Preaching* has often been used as a textbook in preaching courses. In such settings, it has helped to clarify and to bridge the gap between those whose preaching and hermeneutics tend to be more traditional—mostly white males—and the various minorities who tend to read Scripture in a different way. Significantly, the book appears to have been used equally by minority and majority preachers and students. Secondly, we repeatedly receive reports to the effect that the most helpful sections in *Liberation Preaching* are those in which we give concrete examples of how the interpretation of specific biblical texts may be enriched or corrected. For the first of these reasons, while *Liberation Preaching* was intentionally addressed primarily to white male preachers and students of preaching, this new book has been written keeping in mind a much wider group of readers, and seeking to enrich the preaching of minority and women preachers as well as of white males. For the second reason, we have enlarged the number of references to specific passages, and how they may be interpreted from a liberating perspective.

This has its price. We must confess that, after the publication of *Liberation Preaching*, we had to "retire" quite a few sermons and Bible studies. The publication of *The Liberating Pulpit* will require that an even larger number be withdrawn from circulation!

But the price also has its rewards. The very act of "retiring" those older sermons and studies forced us to turn to other biblical texts, and thus to be enriched both in our preaching and in our lives. We trust that the forced "retirement" of this new batch will have a similar salutary effect.

To conclude, a word of gratitude. We must first of all thank the countless preachers and students who have used *Liberation Preaching*, and who have given us words of encouragement as well as suggestions as to how to improve this new version. We must also thank the numerous professors of homiletics who have done likewise. Finally, special thanks to Pacific School of Religion, whose invitation to deliver the Earl Lectures in 1990 provided us the opportunity for much of the reflection that has gone into this revision—particularly for chapter five, much of which is the result of those lectures.

Decatur, GA
June 21, 1993

I

A New Way of Doing Theology

Many important theological developments in the latter half of the twentieth century have made a mark. It is still too early to tell which of them will prove to be most significant in years to come, and into the twenty-first century. It is already clear, however, that when future historians of theology refer to our age, they will have to speak of a time when new voices began to be heard in theology. Until relatively recent times, it was taken for granted that the cutting edge of theology was in the North Atlantic, and that the leading figures in the theological scene were males. That has changed drastically in the last few decades. An increasing number of women are active, both among the ordained and among professional theological scholars. Third World theologians are making themselves felt, not only in their own nations and on issues having to do with missiology, but throughout the world, and on subjects that cover the entire gamut of theological discourse. In the so-called developed world, which comprises the traditional centers of theological inquiry, ethnic minorities are also making themselves felt, and making contributions which all must take into account.

Obviously, this has much to do with the changing demographics of the Christian Church. Numerically, Christianity is losing ground in its former strongholds of the North Atlantic, and rapidly gaining in Asia, Africa, and Latin America. Already at the Second Vatican Council, the majority of bishops represented churches in the so-called under-developed world. The Roman Catholic Church in Latin America, which had long seemed little more than a dead and retrograde hierarchical structure, has shown amazing signs of vitality, and in many places has become the prime vehicle for the expression of the hopes of the masses. In the same continent, Protestantism, particularly in its Pentecostal forms, is also showing enormous growth—to the point that in several countries it is estimated that Protestants are the majority of believers, or nearly so. In the United States, most of the denominations that are showing significant numerical growth are precisely the ones whose constituency generally belongs to the lower echelons of society. And, if there is any growth in "mainline" denominations, this is taking place mostly among their African-American, Latino, and Asian constituencies.

A growing number of people in these groups have rejected the self-image imposed on them. If one takes as an example international colonialism, it has been shown that the colonizers need to justify their enterprise by developing a theory of their cultural superiority, and selling that view to the colonized. For a while, overwhelmed by the power of the colonizers, generations of the colonized may believe what they are told about themselves— their lack of responsibility and organizational skills, their emotionalism, their scarce cultural creativity, etc. But eventually, through a process which takes different shape in various situations, they come to the realization that they do not have to accept the self-image which has been imposed on them by the colonizers.[1] This process, which has spelled the death of the international colonial empires of the nineteenth century, is also taking place in societies such as ours. It happens among those who have been the internal colonies of our society—the poor, African-Americans, Latinos, Asian Americans, Native Americans, and women. It is on the toil of such people, and of the colonized overseas, that much of the wealth of the North Atlantic has been built. And yet those people, who have produced so much wealth, receive the smallest share of it. Therefore, the change in self-image on their part is not a purely psychological or internal matter, but one which demands basic structural changes in the ordering of our society.

Not all people who have come to this awareness belong to the church. Many have left it precisely because they perceive it as part of the very structure of oppression against which they must rebel. And we must admit that such a view is amply justified, when we remember for instance how Christianity was used to take the land from Native Americans and then from Mexicans, how it justified slavery, how few Christian leaders protested against the internment of Japanese Americans during the Second World War, and how the Bible has been used to keep women in a subservient role. At the other extreme, there are many members of these various groups who, out of their Christian faith, refuse to join the movement towards a new self-image or to demand their rights. Many have been taught that it is unchristian to rock the boat, or that if they are humble here on earth they will be rewarded in heaven, or that they should be content to be of service to others and not claim positions of leadership.

14

Between these two extremes, a growing number of people have come to the conclusion that the movement towards a new and fuller self-image does not contradict their Christian faith. Quite the contrary. Their faith is deepened and made more dynamic and more relevant through the development of a greater sense of their own powers and possibilities. In turn, this new sense is deeply rooted in their faith commitment.

Joining these two commitments is not an easy matter. Often, portions of the liberation movements themselves have taken the shape of a rebellion against a Christian faith and tradition that have been quite oppressive. Thus, those who seek to keep the two together are led to reinterpret much of the Christian faith and tradition. Biblical texts which have been adduced to support slavery, oppression, and the subjugation of women are reread and reinterpreted. Doctrines which have been used for similar purposes are also reformulated. And, since practically every traditional doctrine and every traditional reading of Scripture have been used in such fashion, what is required is no less than an entire rereading of both Scripture and tradition.

All of this rereading has lead to the most significant and promising theological development of our time: that some of the most creative theology is being done from the perspective of those who have been traditionally powerless in society and voiceless in the church. In the United States, this means African Americans, Hispanics, Asian Americans, and others. In Latin America, Asia, and Africa, it means those who have long been the subjects of colonialism, economic and political as well as ecclesiastical. In societies which worship youth, it means the aged. All over the world, it means women.

More and more, theology is being done from the perspective of the traditionally powerless as they experience the empowerment of the gospel, not only in an inner sense, but also in the sense that it compels and enables them to strive for justice. In rejecting the traditional interpretation of the Christian message, they refuse to leave the gospel in the hands of the powerful, to be used for their purposes, and insist that a proper interpretation of Scripture is freeing rather than oppressive. It is the entire gamut of theologies emerging from such circumstances—African-American, Latin American, Asian, feminist, womanist, mujerista, etc.—that we call "liberation theology" (or, even better, "liberation theologies").

The History of Subconscious Oppression

All of these theologies suggest that much of traditional theology has carried a hidden—and sometimes not so hidden—agenda of oppression. This is not to say that the powerful have deliberately set out to interpret the Bible in an oppressive way. The truth is much more subtle than that. What actually takes place is an unconscious process through which the values, goals, and interests of those in power are read into Scripture and expressed in supposedly universal theology.

Take for instance what happened in the early centuries of the Christian church. At first, most Christians belonged to the lower classes. Their opponents said that they were uncouth and unlearned, and that their teaching made no sense. A great deal of the Christian literature of the first four centuries seeks to respond to that challenge by showing that Christianity agrees with the best of Greek philosophy and Roman law. Apologists such as Justin, Clement of Alexandria, and Origen claimed that the Christian doctrine of life after death was similar to the Greek theory of the immortality of the soul, and that the God of the Church was the same as the Supreme Idea of Beauty of Plato, or the Prime Unmoved Mover of Aristotle. Other apologists—notably, Tertullian—argued that Christianity stood for the same moral principles as those embodied in the best of Roman law—and that therefore, when Roman law persecuted Christians, it was in fact acting against its own best instincts. As an effort to communicate the gospel to those outside the church, such responses are quite understandable. But eventually Christians themselves began to think that Greek philosophy and Roman law spoke a clearer word about God and the divine purposes than did the Bible itself. By the time Constantine came to power, in the early fourth century, and he and his successors embraced Christianity, it was possible for them to do so without rejecting many of the values of the "best" Greco-Roman society.

The conversion of Constantine, and the support which most of his successors gave to the church, accelerated the process. Eusebius of Caesarea wrote a *Church History* which made it appear that the only reasons why the Empire had persecuted the church were grave misunderstandings and the maliciousness of some rulers—when in fact many of those who led the worst persecutions were among the ablest statesmen and most just rulers who ever governed the Empire. Eusebius's interpretation of past events was biased because he was convinced that God had created the Empire and the Church for each other, that now in Constantine they had come together, and that their previous opposition was an unfortunate mistake. For Eusebius, Constantine was a new King David, raised up by God. Significantly, to this day the commonly held view of the early persecutions is that of Eusebius: if the emperors had really known what Christianity was all about, they would not have persecuted the church.

The Book of Revelation, which spoke of Rome in a rather uncomplimentary fashion, was shunned, and Eusebius himself had doubts about its inclusion in the canon of the New Testament.[2] The ritual of Christian worship began to imitate the formalities of the imperial court, with all their distinctions between various levels in the civil hierarchy. Christ was depicted as sitting on a heavenly throne, in a posture which resembled that of the

16

emperors on their thrones. Even the cross was often studded with precious gems. Anything to obscure the fact that the One whom the church worshiped was a poor carpenter from Galilee, who had been condemned to death as an outlaw by Roman authorities.

Again, this was not a conscious process. Indeed, when reading the documents of the time, one comes across repeated protestations that what is being taught and done in the church is exactly what the apostles taught and did. The "faith of the fathers" became the watchword of orthodoxy. But the "fathers" were for the most part seen as bishops who sat on thrones, very much like the Emperor in Constantinople and the images of Christ in heaven.

There were protests against this. The Donatists broke away from the church and eventually were put down by sheer military force. At another level, the development of monasticism was also a sort of protest. Since the church had embraced the values of the surrounding society, these women and men (in Egypt there seem to have been twice as many female monastics as there were male)[3] felt that the best way for them to reject those values was to live in seclusion, preferably in the desert. This feeling was so widespread that soon travelers said that the desert was as populated as a city. Others, while embracing the monastic attitude toward the prevailing values of society, continued their active involvement in the life of the church and often collided with the powerful. These were the great saints of the fourth and fifth centuries: Athanasius, Ambrose, Jerome, Macrina, Basil, John Chrysostom, etc. Many of these we shall have occasion to quote later on, when we deal with resources from the early Christian tradition.

The usually unconscious process of adapting Christian teaching to the views and interests of the powerful did not end with Constantine and his successors. It has continued, for instance, in the manner in which the oppression and persecution of Jews has received religious and theological sanction. In the history of the Western Hemisphere it has appeared again and again in the taking of the land from its original inhabitants, in the destruction of ancient civilizations, in the annexation of Mexican territories by the U.S., in black slavery on both continents, etc., etc.

The oppressive use of supposedly Christian doctrine has repeatedly been pointed out. However, what we often fail to realize is that most of the people who did this were sincere in their beliefs. This was particularly clear in the case of the conquest and colonization of the Western Hemisphere by European invaders. Already in 1992, on the occasion of the quincentennial of the so-called discovery of America, there was much discussion of the atrocities committed by the Spanish and others as they came to the Western Hemisphere to serve God and themselves.[4] Throughout the latter part of the twentieth century, and well into the twenty-first, other quincentennials will constantly remind us of those events—the founding of several cities in the Caribbean, the "discovery" of Florida, the conquests of Mexico and Peru, the founding of St. Augustine, etc. We will hear and read of massacres, of incredible cruelty and exploitation, of the destruction of precious manuscripts and works of art, of the sacking of temples, and much more. We will read and hear of these things, and we will be properly shocked. But we will probably avoid the full impact of these stories by forgetting that the people who committed such atrocities were deeply sincere and committed Christians. Even worse, they often convinced themselves that those acts which we now deplore were done in the service of God. It was not that they consciously decided to interpret the Bible in such a way that it supported exploitation. It was rather that, from their perspective, a different interpretation was highly unlikely. And, since their views were reflected in the centers of authority within the church, their interpretation became normative and was passed on as authoritative, not only to later generations among the powerful, but also to the powerless, who were left with the alternative of either acquiescing to exploitation or rejecting Christianity.

That is precisely the great danger and even the tragedy of a theology and a biblical interpretation that is done exclusively—or almost exclusively—from positions of relative power: the colonizers vis-à-vis the colonized, men vis-à-vis women, the North Atlantic vis-à-vis the Third World, etc.

Now, however, many among the traditionally powerless are asking the basic question of whether or not the manner in which the Bible has been interpreted by the powerful is accurate. This is the "ideological suspicion" of which we shall have much more to say. Could it not be that a biblical interpretation, so to speak, "from below," would uncover dimensions of the biblical message that have often been ignored?

The Main Biblical Perspective

Many have argued that an interpretation of the Bible done by the powerless would be no less biased and determined by self-interest than is the current one done by the powerful. Why trade one such interpretation for another? Nothing would really be gained. The response of liberation theologians is clear at this point and needs to be understood before any real progress can be made in the appreciation of liberation theology for preaching. It has to do with the perspective of the Bible itself.

If the major portion of the Bible records the perspective of those who, in their own social situation, are the powerless and oppressed, if it is their perspective on the activity of God that is given us by Scripture, then surely a more accurate interpretation of the biblical word can be gained by those who currently stand in a parallel place in our own societies than by those who are powerful. This response should be examined in some detail.

First of all, is it true that most of the Bible reflects the perspective of the powerless? Surely this is the case. The people of Israel begin their organized life as a band of runaway slaves, escaping the oppression of Pharaoh. Even the Promised Land they finally attain is an insecure piece of geography, at the crossroads of trade routes and constantly a battleground for the mighty empires that surround Israel. The only times when ancient Israel had a semblance of independent national life are in brief periods when these empires—Egypt to the west, or whatever is the current name of the peoples to the northeast in the great Mesopotamian and Persian area, and finally Macedonia, Syria, and Rome—are in disarray internally and cannot exercise their usual demand for tribute or subservience.

Almost perversely, God chose a people weak and small in number, in preference to the mighty nations of the earth (Deut. 7:7). Thus Israel could then be clear that the power is God's power, and not Israel's own strength (Deut. 8:1-20). In grateful response to God, Israel ought then to be obedient to God's will as expressed in the law. Relying on her own strength, which was tempting whenever the nation seemed to be strong and independent, inevitably brought about faithlessness and disobedience, which God then punished and cured by removing Israel's apparent power.   The slaves escaping from Egypt surely had a different perspective on God's activity and character than did their Egyptian pursuers. The kings of Israel often forgot the Law when the nation was strong and prosperous. Even mighty David was rebuked by Nathan the prophet (II Sam. 12:1-15). David's greatness was seen in his response to the rebuke, in his hearing of the Word of God to him from the prophet. Other kings did not listen so well. King Jeroboam much preferred his own court priests, who told him what he wished to hear, rather than listen to Amos, the rough shepherd from south of the border who brought God's authentic word to him (Amos 7:10-17; see also II Chron. 18).

This is the pattern throughout much of the Old Testament. The powerful nations are overthrown by small Israel when Israel is obedient. The powerful within Israel are rebuked by the seemingly powerless prophets. It is astonishing that the Old Testament records all of this. The Old Testament is not only our sacred Scripture. It is also a national history. Such histories normally glorify the nation. All difficulties are due to evil enemies, never to sinfulness within the nation itself. National heroes are models of perfection, and have their weaknesses overlooked. That is the general plan of secular national histories. But the Old Testament is quite different, and in this difference is seen the revelation of God. The official records are included, but the minority report of the prophets is even more in evidence. Much of what has been preserved by Israel is the perspective of the powerless over against the viewpoint of the powerful. Included also are the repentant powerful who have learned through their own bitter experience that God is the defender of the poor and oppressed and not the supporter of the unjust, whether they be kings or nations.

Yet this does not mean that God prefers those who maintain a low opinion

19

of themselves. Too often humility has been interpreted in this manner. Rather, God seems to choose those who have been made to feel like outcasts, those who are powerless and marginal, and then gives them a new sense of self-worth. God vindicates them in the eyes of their former oppressors. This theme of vindication of the powerless is a constant one in the Old Testament (see especially I Sam. 2:1-10). It is to be contrasted with the sinful arrogance of the powerful who believe themselves secure in their own strength (see Ps.73). Humility and weakness alone are not enough for faithfulness. In the Old Testament, faithful humility is combined in the powerless with the belief that God will indeed be their strength and that they can therefore hold their heads up very high, especially in the face of their oppressors.

In the New Testament, we are not dealing with a national history, but rather with that of an emerging community and its development into an institution. Yet the same pattern continues. Those who hear the gospel gladly are by and large not the powerful within the society of Israel. Rather, they are the fisherfolk, the women, the poor, and those who are marginalized because of their occupations: the tax collectors and the harlots.

The early church, as it moved into gentile circles, continued to attract those who were unimportant and even powerless, rather than the elite among the Greeks (I Cor. 1:26-31). Yet there were some exceptions. Within Judaism, and within the New Testament, Paul is a prime example of one who comes from the situation of the powerful. He was clearly among the educated and respected within Judaism (Phil. 3:4-6). We know also that Paul was a Roman citizen, which gave him status within the empire itself. Paul can be classified among the "repentant powerful," rather like King David. For him, believing in this "nobody" Jesus meant joining a group that was totally unlike his own secure social position. In joining this community of outcasts, he agreed that the future lay with this marginal group and not with the trimmings of prestige and power to which he had been accustomed (Phil. 3:7-9).

Simon Magus is another example of a powerful person who becomes a Christian. But it takes the fisherman, Simon Peter, to make clear to him that his understanding of the faith is very faulty. Simon Magus evidently then repents and hears the gospel authentically (Acts 8:9-24), but the New Testament does not give us any glimpse into his life after this encounter, such as we are given into the life of Paul.

The New Testament, just as the Old, shows the people of God with all of their faults. We are not presented with an ideal group of perfect people. It is precisely the weakness of the people that allows the surpassing power of God to be seen. And when the people are faithful to such a God, these weak ones are filled with a power that astonishes even the powerful outside the church.

When there was the danger that some Christians might forget this, and

20

begin discriminating against others from lower echelons of society, Paul put it quite bluntly:

> Consider your own call, brothers and sisters: not many of you were wise by human standards, not many were powerful, not many were of noble birth. But God chose what is foolish in the world to shame the wise; God chose what is weak in the world to shame the strong; God chose what is low and despised in the world, things that are not, to reduce to nothing things that are, so that no one might boast in the presence of God (I Cor. 1:26-29).

The supreme example of this is, of course, Jesus himself. In terms of worldly power and prestige, surely he was an outsider. He was born in a stable, the child of poor parents who were being moved around by an alien government. He grew up in an obscure village where the mighty need not pay any attention to him. And yet, in this One, God was incarnate. From our human perspective, it would have made more sense for the divine incarnation to be in the form of a king or a priest, or at least one of the elite of Jerusalem. Yet God the Son chose the form of a servant (Phil. 2:6-8), one of the powerless ones, even as God had chosen Israel, a weak nation. The cross shows the culmination of such a life, with all of its weakness and marginality. The resurrection shows the vindication by God in the most radical form.

God has a proclivity for speaking the word through the powerless. The whole Bible bears witness to this. Is this an accident, or is it an essential element of the gospel itself? Is there something about God's word that can best be heard and spoken by the powerless? We would say there is indeed. And in this we are supported by the words of Jesus: "I thank you, Father . . . because you have hidden these things from the wise and the intelligent and revealed them to infants" (Luke 10:21). The powerful have a difficult time hearing God accurately. Their choice seems to be hearing God's word to them through some apparently powerless person—Nathan, Amos, Simon Peter, Jesus—or not hearing it at all. In our own day, the pattern continues. The powerless have a more ready access to an authentic understanding of the gospel than do the powerful. The powerful need to hear the word through voices they have rejected in their own society. Liberation theology is an understanding of the gospel arising precisely in the midst of such traditionally rejected voices.

Some Basic Traits and Themes

Probably the greatest misrepresentation of liberation theology is that it deals primarily or exclusively with the subject of liberation—or, even worse, of violence and revolution. It is true that these themes are important for liberation theology, which often begins from the experience of institution-

21

alized violence—a violence which is often unseen and unrecognized by those who suffer from it. Yet liberation theologians refuse to limit themselves to the themes most directly and obviously connected with their struggles. This is one of its most puzzling characteristics for those who look at it from the outside, and therefore there is little wonder that it has been misrepresented on this point. Liberation theology is not a theology *about* liberation which is then content to leave all the other theological themes to traditional theology. On the contrary, it is convinced that its insights have a bearing on every single doctrine of the Christian faith, and that it is therefore a legitimate theology. "Feminist theology is *not* about women. It is about God."[5] And "when black people sing, preach, and tell stories about their struggle, one fact is clear: they are not dealing simply with themselves. . . . It is this affirmation of transcendence that prevents Black Theology from being reduced merely to the cultural history of the black people."[6]

Liberation theology deals with every theme in Christian theology, from the doctrine of God to that of the last things.[7] But it deals with each and all of these themes from the perspective of its particular struggle and action.

At the same time, it is also clear that each form of liberation theology has its own starting point, its own issues that make it unique. We have learned from bitter experience that most often what passes for "universal" is little more than a projection of the values, self-image, and interests of a powerful group that has somehow become normative. In a white racist society, an "average" human being is depicted as white. In a sexist society, male domination seems normal, and men take for granted that the fruit of their philosophical and theological reflection has nothing to do with their gender or their position of dominance. Therefore, it is important to underline that all theology reflects a concrete experience and perspective. As Mexican theologian Raúl Vidales has written, "There has never been a 'universal' theology, and even less has there been a neutral one."[8] Therefore, although there are many points of contact, and certainly a common perspective, joining the various theologies of liberation, it is important to keep in mind this emphasis on concreteness, in order to avoid the temptation of becoming a preacher of "universal"—and therefore abstract—liberation, or of someone else's liberation.

Precisely because of this concreteness and particularity, each theology of liberation has its own points of departure, and these are closely related to the nature of its struggle. It is for this reason that Third World theologies often begin from the perspective of the poor, and emphasize economic oppression and its structures—both international and domestic. Theologies of liberation that reflect the struggle of culturally suppressed minorities often begin from the experience of cultural identity and its recovery. Likewise, feminist, womanist and mujerista theologies tend to center their attention on issues related to gender oppression—although womanist theology also places issues of race at the center of its concern, and mujerista theology adds the dimension of culture.

This emphasis on particularity may prove disturbing to many. Some would still insist on the goal of a 'universal' theology, and thus bemoan the 'fragmentation' of theology. This is one of the criticisms most often levelled at liberation theologies by white male theologians who still refuse to see that their own theology is just as concrete and particular as any other. Even among theologians of liberation, the attempt sometimes appears to bring about unity by creating a sort of hierarchy of struggles. This became apparent in some of the earlier meetings of Latin American liberation theologians with proponents of North American black theology: while the former claimed that the major issue was poverty and class struggle, the latter insisted that it was race and racism. Or at a meeting of ethnic minority theologians, when an African-American woman was speaking, some sought to force her to declare whether she thought that issues of gender were more important than race, or vice versa. All of this represents an attempt to deprive liberation theologies of their concreteness and particularity.

On the other hand, this does not mean that each struggle for liberation must go its own separate way, and that there are no points of contact among the various theologies coming out of such struggles. On the contrary, as Christian theologians we know that evil is ultimately one, even though it takes many different shapes. In the "big picture," our struggle is not against classism, against racism, against ageism, or against sexism. Our struggle is against Evil, and therefore, in spite of the many shapes it takes, it is a single struggle. It is on this basis that we frequently find points of contact among the various theologies of liberation, and that where we find ourselves working at cross-purposes we must pause lest we find ourselves to be instruments of Evil perpetrated against others. Furthermore, theologians who represent various struggles for liberation are becoming increasingly aware that quite often the apparent opposition among their various causes is the result of a policy of "divide and conquer" implemented by those who still hold the power to form public opinion and even to mold theological debate.

Another common characteristic of liberation theologies is that the main category with which they work is that of history. A significant segment of traditional theology deals with truth understood in terms of changelessness and universality. Others seem to believe that the basic category of the biblical message is that of law, doing what is proper and orderly.[9] But liberation theologians know that supposedly "universal" truth is too often the projection of the particular views and interests of the powerful, that changelessness is a value espoused by those who benefit from the status quo, for whom change would be threatening, and that law is most cherished by those who have the civil law and order on their side. As we read the Bible, what we see in it is not so much a book of eternal truths, nor a book of rules, as a book of history. In the Bible, truth is not something that "is," in the sense in which Parmenides used that word, but rather something that happens. And laws are given, not to stifle that happening, but to foster it. This is why James Cone says that "In the Bible revelation is inseparable from history and faith. History is the arena in which God's revelation takes place."[10] And Letty M. Russell speaks both for feminist theology and for other theologies of liberation when she asserts that "Most liberation theologies are written from the modern point of view that both humanity and the world are to be understood as historical, as both changing and changeable."[11]

This understanding of history, however, has to be clarified. History is not simply the narration of past events. History is a project, both divine and human, for the redemption of God's creation. "If theology is really to speak meaningfully about the mediating point between the 'is' and the 'ought' of human life," says a feminist theologian, "then it takes as its base the entire human project."[12] And Gustavo Gutiérrez: "Indeed, if human history is above all else an opening to the future, then it is a task, a political occupation, through which [we open ourselves] to the gift which gives history its transcendent meaning: the full and definitive encounter with the Lord and with others."[13] James Cone agrees: "By making revelation a historical happening, the Bible makes faith something other than an ecstatic feeling in moments of silent prayer, or an acceptance of inerrant propositions. Faith is the community's response to God's act of liberation. It is saying Yes to God and No to oppressors."[14]

Liberation and Liberalism

At this point, it is important to point out that liberation theologies are not part of a spectrum that goes from conservative to liberal to liberation. Sometimes, liberation theologians find that those who have most difficulty in understanding them are not those who call themselves "conservative," but those who claim to be "liberal." There are many reasons for this, but at least two must be mentioned in this context. The first of these is that much of liberal theology, in spite of its claim to universality and openness, developed as the theological expression of the experiences and interests of males in the growing middle classes in the North Atlantic, particularly during the late nineteenth century and the early twentieth. These ties with a particular segment of the human community, particularly when they remain hidden, make it difficult for liberal theologians to understand and accept the concreteness of particular liberation theologies. What is typical of liberal theology is the notion that the value of Scripture lies in the fact that it points to certain essential principles, and that theology then seeks to interpret Scripture so as to find them. A typical case is the famous liberal theology summary of the message of the Sermon on the Mount as the "Fatherhood of God,

24

and the infinite value of the human soul." Even
...er-specific language, this sort of summary, in its aim
, historical specificity. In our own day, psychological
...ised for the same purpose.

...theology often lacks a strong sense of the Word of God,
...beyond the present order. This is partly because liberal
...agree with the "best" of society around it, and therefore
...such a Word. Liberation theologies, on the other hand,
...selves struggling against the supposedly "best" in their own
...erefore for them the notion of such a Word of God is crucial.
... liberation theologians sometimes find that the "conserva-
...er to them than are the "liberals."

...s a third point at which liberation theology parts company with
...ogy; liberal theologians, and liberal church members, often find
...or even impossible to recognize their own oppression. And, until
...at, they cannot really understand the very nature of liberation
...Many white, middle-class liberal Christians in this country readily
a... ...tantly feel a sense of guilt for their position of affluence in a world
beset by problems of hunger and poverty. Obviously, there is ample reason
for such a sense of guilt. Yet often such guilt leads to the conclusion that we
are guilty because we voluntarily chose such affluence. We created the
problem and we can therefore alter the situation. The feeling of guilt is
acceptable to us as long as we can also have the sense that we, unlike the
oppressed we wish to help, are free and independent members of society.
We can decide to assist those who are downtrodden to help them attain the
status we have. It is not so pleasant to think of ourselves as both guilty and
powerless. It is difficult to accommodate the thought that the vast majority
of us who see ourselves as free are really the captives of the same structures
and forces that cause the poverty we wish to eliminate. Yet this thought is
essential if we are to see how liberation theology can relate to our preaching
and to many of our churches.

Justo once had the opportunity to discuss issues of world hunger with a
number of congregations and adult Sunday school classes in mainline
denominations. Invariably, as the situation of hunger throughout the world
was described, the response was, "What can we do?" In a way, that is typical
of the self-image of middle-class liberals in the North Atlantic. We believe
that we can "do" something about everything. If something does not happen, it is our fault. We can fix it. And it certainly is true that, as Christians,
we must do all we can in order to "fix" that which must be corrected. Yet, it
is also true that most of us are less powerful and less free than we think we
are. One of our constitutive myths is precisely that we are free, that we have
the power to change, not only ourselves, but also society around us. To
discover that we too are oppressed, that our freedom too is curtailed by

structures which dominate and even oppress us, would be shattering to most of us. Yet, until we make that discovery we cannot begin to be really free, and to join the struggle for the radical liberation, not only of ourselves, but of the whole of God's creation.

All Are Bound Together

A very important point to keep in mind is that ultimately there is only one liberation, and that therefore there is only one oppression. In a sense, this is a theological statement, made on the basis of faith. The basic tenet of the Christian faith is that the victory belongs to Jesus, and that through that victory he is our Redeemer. "For there is no other name under heaven given among mortals by which we must be saved" (Acts 4:12, NRSV). But this also implies that the powers of oppression which Jesus has defeated and is defeating are in the final analysis only one. There is only one Victor, and there is only one Enemy.

Although this statement is based on faith, observation of the present world order seems to confirm it. Racism in the United States is not unrelated to apartheid in South Africa, and the two are supported by the same economic structures which lead to the dispossession of peasants in Brazil and in the Philippines. The exploitation of women, their stereotyping into sex roles or into Christmas trees on which successful males display the signs of their success, is also part of the same picture. The fear which white males in the United States show toward their African- and Hispanic-American counterparts is the other side of the coin of the way in which women are stereotyped in our society. And minority men are often led by their own oppression to oppress minority women. All of this is closely related to our present consumer society, where human beings are seen as either means of production or agents of consumption, and where the poor are valued according to how much they produce, while the rich are valued according to how much they consume.

As a consequence of this unity of the oppressive system, to strike a blow for any particular kind of liberation is to strike a blow against the system itself. And this is the reason why it is possible to preach and to practice liberation even though one is a white male middle-class preacher in the United States. It is possible, because the liberation of the middle-class will eventually be part of the entire process of liberation of the human race. But it is also difficult, because the middle-class lives precisely by the myth that it is not oppressed. It is easier to convince a successful businessman that he is an oppressor, than to convince him that he is oppressed. The reason for that should be quite obvious. If that businessman becomes convinced that he is an oppressor, he still has that sense of power which is so important for his own image of himself. But if he is told that he is oppressed, this means that all the tokens of his success, with which the system rewards him, are little more than the price paid for his enslavement. He is little more than more meat for the grinder of production. And it is difficult for a middle-class male to admit this.

Furthermore, it is difficult because the price to be paid for such an admission could be exceedingly high. A successful businessman may admit that he is psychologically oppressed, and go to a therapist seeking a solution; but to admit the kind of oppression to which we are referring here may lead to radical changes in life-style and to eventual expulsion from the middle class. In a way, such a businessman finds himself in a situation similar to that of a sergeant in the army of a military dictatorship: the sergeant seems to be an important personage in his own village, but if he ever decides to leave the army he will find himself under a duress even greater than that which mere civilians suffer. Therefore, it is very difficult for such a sergeant to confess to himself that, important though he seems, he too is oppressed, jointly with the rest of the population.

This is not the same as to say that we are all oppressed in one way or another and thus we can be rid of our sense of guilt. That will not do at all, though such an attitude often occurs when we discover our own powerlessness. Nor is it legitimate to spiritualize the meaning of bondage so that some of us are captives of poverty and others of sin, but ultimately we are all in the same situation. This would imply that we need not deal with our role as oppressors at all, since in the last analysis we are all oppressed. The reality of racism and the evils of injustice must be dealt with. The sense of guilt on the consciences of the comfortable must be nurtured and not assuaged.

Yet the truth remains. We are not the free people we often think we are. The bondage under which we live is subtle, and we are sufficiently rewarded that we do not notice our lack of freedom. In the painful transitions that a global economy creates, as layoffs have occurred, many managerial and professional people, who thought themselves safe from the insecurity of domination by economic structures they could not control, have learned the harsh reality of their situation. The structures that buy or lease land in the Third World and displace people, causing them to become part of the inhuman slums of the sprawling cities, are the same structures that govern much of our lives as well. From products to pricing, from values to self-images, from advertising to television programming, our lives and those of our children are determined in ways that would startle our great-grandparents. If we try to alter things we discover that even regulatory agencies and government itself are strongly influenced by these same interests. Change is neither easy nor always possible. Our own employment may well be governed or at least financed by the same systems, and if we cry out too loudly, we are made aware that it is not wise.

What does all of this have to do with liberation theology? If we take it

27

seriously, it has a great deal to do with it. If we can become aware of the social, political, and economic systems that control our lives, we may then find ourselves on the same side of the struggle as those who are the outcasts of those systems. We can then speak from our own experience of bondage and of the problems and frustrations in seeking to be free. We can know what it means to come to consciousness about our own exploitation, even though we fully recognize that our bondage has been quite comfortable. Only then can we really seek to be free. This experience of a white, male, middle-class minister discovering his own oppression, and on that basis joining the struggle for liberation, has been well expressed by Richard Shaull:

> In the midst of the turmoil of the sixties, I was forced to face the fact that, for many of the most sensitive of a younger generation, *the American dream had become a nightmare.* Institutions that had offered me and my generation the hope of a better future, were now experienced as structures of death. . . . The American dream had died, not only for many others, but *for myself as well.* . . . In the midst of the collapse of the old order, I see signs of a new world taking shape; I begin to perceive and to work for a new future.[15]

Once we have acknowledged our own lack of freedom, we can find ourselves learning much about our own struggle from those whom we charitably tried to help before. They can become our teachers, rather than we theirs. The poor, precisely because they are at the margins of the system, may well know more about its actual working than we who are kept within it.

Within the church there is great possibility for such a conversation because the church has within its membership all races, economic groups, and social conditions, and is spread over the face of the earth. Yet our local congregations fail to take constant advantage of this truly catholic character of the church and, in their own congregational life, fail to reflect it.

Liberation theology is significant for us when we seek to become free from actual oppressive structures that bind us. Wherever we, who think ourselves powerful, find that we are in fact bound, such a theology can inspire us to have the courage to challenge and to act as the redeemed children of God, as those who are indeed not conformed to this world.

For most of us in this country, liberation theology, to be useful and authentic, demands a kind of double personality. Our consciences must continue to remind us of evil from which we benefit while others suffer. Our awareness of this must increase and not decrease. Our affluence, even though it hardly seems such in comparison to richer neighbors, still is more than our share of the world's resources. Besides this, however, most of us find ourselves in multiple roles. We may be the powerful by race if we are white, yet among the powerless if we are women. We may be part of a powerless group if we are in an ethnic minority, yet if we are well educated and employed, we join the powerful in that category. Even within the family structure, the child is often the last victim of those who have no one else over whom to rule and yet are oppressed themselves. Our tendency is to claim only one part of our identity, to think of ourselves always as part of an oppressed group or to think of ourselves always as the powerful. A much more creative dynamic is possible when we claim both parts of our identity, and the liberation given by the gospel can nurture a constant interior dialogue within our own lives. It can also open our lives to a far greater dialogue in the world around us. Then liberation theology can speak to us and to our congregations, making clear and judging our roles as oppressors, but also making clear and freeing us from whatever powers bind us, even those forces that bind us into the role of oppressors in the wider society.

II

Difficulties
in Hearing the Text

We are convinced that the main task of the preacher is to listen anew to the biblical text, and to interpret contemporary life in the light of that text. In our view, this is much more important to preaching than matters of style, organization, illustration, etc. Such concerns, though serious, are secondary to the issue of interpretation. For this reason, this chapter and the next two will deal with the question of biblical interpretation. In the present chapter, we shall discuss some of the obstacles which impede a liberating interpretation, and in the others we shall deal with some resources for overcoming those obstacles.

Sola Scriptura

One of the main principles of the Protestant Reformation was that of *sola Scriptura*—the sole authority of Scripture in questions of faith. The Reformers themselves did not fully agree on the scope and application of this principle. Some, like Luther, meant by it that anything which was contrary to the clear words of Scripture should be rejected, while traditions that did not contradict the Bible could—and normally should—be retained. Zwingli and others went much farther and sought to do away with anything that was not clearly supported by Scripture. But in spite of these differences, all agreed that the reason why the Reformation was needed was that, to a greater or lesser degree, the tradition of the church made it difficult, if not impossible, to read the Bible correctly. Thus, in a sense, the Reformation of the sixteenth century was an attempt to rediscover the biblical word, somehow obscured by its traditional interpretation.

As is well known, this gave rise to bitter controversy. It is difficult for us today to understand the real nature of that controversy, because we have repeatedly been told that it was simply a matter of the relative authority of tradition vis-à-vis Scripture, and at present both Protestants and Roman Catholics tend to agree that there is a certain priority to Scripture. But those who opposed the Reformers in the sixteenth century did not see matters in this light. To them what was being attacked was not simply a tradition that was clearly distinct from the Bible. They were so used to reading the Bible as they had been taught by generations of interpreters that any questioning of that interpretation seemed to be a questioning of Scripture itself. Therefore the thrust of their argument was not, as has so often been said, that tradition was above Scripture, or that it added something to the Bible, but rather that the two were so closely entwined that to doubt the traditional interpretation of the Bible was to doubt the authority of both the Bible and tradition.

In a way, this is a battle that the church always has to fight over and over again. Even those of us who claim to be heirs of the Reformers have been taught to interpret certain texts in a particular way, and are rather reluctant to read them in a different manner. This is true, first of all, of our "canon within the canon." We have learned from our communities of faith that certain texts are more important than others, and we are unwilling to question that selection, or to explore what a different "canon" of preferred texts would entail. We have also learned how to interpret particular texts. We "know," for instance, that in the parable of the Good Samaritan we are to identify with the Samaritan. We "know" that the passage in Romans 1 about justification by faith refers to the manner in which Christ's merits are ascribed to us. We "know" that the passage in I Corinthians 11:29 about those who "eat judgment" for themselves means that before we approach the Table we must make careful confession of our sins and be old enough to have a clear understanding of the meaning of the sacrament. And, since we "know" all these things, we are determined not to allow the biblical text itself to tell us otherwise. Thus, in our interpretation of Scripture, we are not that distant from those in the sixteenth century who opposed the Reformers.

Traditions of interpretation are not ideologically neutral. They do not just happen. On the contrary, they have an agenda. They reflect the perspectives and the interests of the interpreters. And they do this to a degree which is usually in inverse relation to the degree to which the interpreter is conscious of what is taking place. In other words, the less aware the interpreter is of his or her biases, the more surreptitiously they will permeate the interpretation. In the case of issues regarding women, for instance, the most insidious interpretations have not come from those who consciously set out to put women down, but rather from an entire tradition which developed in a society which took for granted that women were inferior human beings, and in which biblical interpreters—almost exclusively male—reflected that bias in their exposition of Scripture.

We are heirs of the ancient theologians, of medieval theologians, of the Reformers, and of the Puritans. To deny such inheritance is to deny our faith. But to claim a historic faith also means to claim one that is constantly moving toward God's future, and therefore we must learn to claim our inheritance in such a way that it is a help rather than a hindrance in our march toward the future. In other words, we must learn to reevaluate and reinterpret what has been handed down to us.

Many of us who have come to this conclusion find something autobiographic in what Juan Luis Segundo calls the "hermeneutic circle," in which there are four basic moments:

> Firstly, there is our way of experiencing reality, which leads us to ideological suspicion. *Secondly* there is the application of our ideological suspicion to the whole ideological superstructure in general and to theology in particular. *Thirdly* there comes a new way of experiencing theological reality that leads us to exegetical suspicion, that is, to the suspicion that the prevailing interpretation of the Bible has not taken important pieces of data into account. *Fourthly* we have our new hermeneutic, that is, our new way of interpreting the fountainhead of our faith (i.e., Scripture) with the new elements at our disposal.[1]

To put these ideas in less terse language, one could say that most of us began with a theological naïveté. We believed, not only that what the Bible said was true, but also that the Bible actually said what our mentors and the tradition before them told us that it said. Then, through a series of episodes, we became conscious of the structures of oppression around and above us, and tried to do something about them. But hardly had we begun to get involved in whatever concern claimed our allegiance, when we were told that what we were doing was unbiblical and antichristian. If ours was a cause of racial justice, we were told that the Bible supported racism. If it was a question of economic justice, we were told that we ought to be concerned about more spiritual matters. If it was a struggle against sexism, we were told that Christian women are to be meek, and that to claim our rights was unchristian pride. At that point, many of our friends and companions saw the need for a choice, and some opted to abandon the church, while others abandoned the particular social issue. Those of us who sought a different alternative were quickly thrust into Segundo's circle. We became suspicious of the biblical exegesis which was being used against us and came to the conclusion that, like the Reformers of old, we must be willing to read the Bible *de novo*. Thus we came to our "new hermeneutic," and began applying it, eventually to come to the joyful discovery that the Bible was much more on our side than we ever dared hope, and that there were throughout the world a host of others who had gone through parallel struggles and had arrived at similar methodologies and conclusions.

To be able to do liberation theology, a person must first have gone through the painful experience of this circle or of another like it. It does not suffice to come in at the last stage, read up on the methodology of liberation exegesis, study the most significant books, and go out to preach liberation.

At this point, an autobiographical note or two may be in order, for as we write these lines both of us can remember "Aha!" experiences which were the beginning of our plunge into the "hermeneutical circle." We say "plunge," because once one is thrust into the hermeneutical suspicion that is central to this circle, there is no stopping. On the contrary, it would seem that the speed at which the circle turns becomes ever more accelerated, as we discover more and more hidden dimensions in the biblical text.

For Justo, the background of his "Aha!" experience is to be found many years ago, when he was a six- or seven-year-old growing up in Cuba. It was Holy Thursday, and the preacher spoke of Peter's denial. "How did people know that Peter was a Christian?" he asked. And his answer was, "because when you have been with Jesus the experience is so overwhelming, and has such a power of transformation, that it shows in your face." After worship, I remember that I sat on a curb just outside the church door, looking at all who came out. I studied their faces one by one, and decided that not one of them, not even the preacher, had been with Jesus!

It was many years later, after I had finished my Ph.D. and was teaching in Puerto Rico, that I came to read that text in a different way. For Holy Week, I had been invited to preach a series of sermons at a large church in the United States. I was worried, because I had never spoken in English before such a large audience. Above all, I was concerned that I would not have the right words or, even more, that because of my Spanish accent I would not be understood. It was while preparing the sermon for Holy Thursday that I came once again to the text about Peter's denial, as it is told in the Gospel of Matthew, and saw something I had never noticed before, even though I had read the text countless times: in Matthew 26:73, the bystanders say to Peter, "Certainly you are also one of them, for your accent betrays you." The reason why they knew that Peter was a Christian was not that his face shone, nor that he showed a particularly placid countenance. The reason why they knew was that he had an accent! He did not speak like the "regular" folk from Jerusalem!

From that point on, it became apparent that what was taking place in the trial and passion of Jesus, as Matthew and the other evangelists tell it, was at least in part a conflict between the established religious authorities in Jerusalem, and the group of Galileans who, under the leadership of Jesus, were now threatening those authorities. As years went by, and with the help of ideas from my friends Virgilio Elizondo (a Roman Catholic from Texas) and Orlando Costas (a Baptist from Puerto Rico), I came to see that the conflict between the center (Jerusalem) and the periphery (Galilee) is paradigmatic for much that has taken place in the history of the church and still takes place today.[2]

For Catherine, the text that was pivotal was Genesis 3:16: the curse on women. While in graduate school, I had read a sermon on that passage written by a pastor in the late nineteenth century, shortly after the discovery of anesthesia. The point he made was that no Christian woman would use anesthesia in childbirth, because God wanted women to suffer pain. I thought that was a strange comment, but filed it away in my mind without finding it significant. Many years later, I was asked to marry a couple, both of whom were faculty members at the college where I taught. The pastor of the bride visited her, and brought her pre-nuptial material from that very conservative tradition. It said that no Christian woman would practice natural childbirth, because that was a means to lessen the pain God had intended for women to suffer. Evidently anesthesia had become acceptable, if needed; but natural childbirth had not. That was in the late 1960s. At that point, I remembered the earlier sermon. Most of the churches I knew would not agree with such interpretations. But those generally liberal churches would agree with another part of the verse, and seek to apply it to women's lives today—the part that says the husband will rule over the wife. Evidently, for many congregations, it was very good to try to eliminate the pain in childbirth, but the subjection of wives must remain. One part of the verse was treated as the result of sin, and its elimination was a good cause; the other part was the way God intended things, and should not be changed.

But the matter did not end there. Once I began to see Genesis 3:16 in a new way, I remembered the curse on the man in Genesis 3:17-19. He is to sweat in order to earn his bread, and the ground will produce thorns and thistles to make it difficult. Yet no church that I knew of opposed air-conditioned offices or tractors for men, nor were weed killers outlawed because of this verse. Yet if the same principles of interpretation had been used on these verses as had traditionally been used on Genesis 3:16, serious questions would have been raised about both of those modern conveniences. There was a basic issue about the role of the gospel and therefore of the church: is it to enforce the curses—the effects of sin—or to announce that the bondage to sin and its effects have been overcome in Christ?

I am sure that if women had done all of the previous biblical interpretation, pain in childbirth and subjection to husbands would have been eliminated or lessened much earlier. But this does not mean there would have been no biases. Perhaps pain in childbirth would have been eliminated, but probably weed killers and air-conditioned offices might have taken a lot longer!

For the person who has gone through the circle, liberation theology is grounded on a basic suspicion. This is what Segundo calls "ideological suspicion," and is present even where it is not explicitly named as such. An African American man involved in the struggle against racism has come up against so many instances of hidden racism that he must regard every statement coming out of a predominantly white society as implicitly racist. A woman who is conscious of the prevailing sexism around her must also suspect every statement made by male-dominated theology of being ideologically sexist. From the point of view of those who have not gone through the same painful experiences, such a man and such a woman may seem unduly belligerent and negative—even paranoid. But the truth of the matter is that the experience of going through the hermeneutic circle is so overwhelming that those who have gone through it cannot but refer everything to that experience.

Perhaps an example taken from an entirely different field may be helpful at this point. When Descartes became suspicious of the data of the senses, he came to the conclusion that the only way in which he could attain trustworthy knowledge was to begin by doubting everything. Anything which could, should be doubted, not for the sake of doubt, but for the sake of knowledge. To many of his critics, this seemed akin to agnosticism. But Descartes was convinced that this universal doubt was necessary in order to attain certainty. Likewise, the "ideological suspicion" of those who are conscious of having experienced oppression, unbelieving and skeptical as it may seem from outside, is the only way we can be sure that we are doing all we can to rid biblical interpretation of its traditionally oppressive bias.

After we have gone through the circle and made it a part of our basic theological outlook, we can once again look at tradition, no longer as that which we have to oppose because it is oppressive, but rather as that which, in our struggle for liberation, we are to reevaluate and reclaim. Tradition then becomes a living reality, in which we discover many kindred spirits whose struggle was akin to ours, but who have been forgotten or obscured by an interpretation which sought to preserve the existing order.

The same is true of the tradition of biblical interpretation. Having learned to read such interpretation with suspicion, we gain new love and respect, first for the Bible, and then for a tradition of which we too are a part, and which we are helping to shape.

Traduttore Traditore

The Italian phrase, *traduttore traditore*—a translator is a traitor—expresses in a nutshell, albeit somewhat mordantly, the dilemma faced by every translator. Languages are not exactly equivalent to each other. Anyone who has good command of more than one language, and has ever tried to translate from one to the other, is well aware that the task of translating involves almost constant choice between various alternatives, and that the finished product expresses, not only the views of the original writer, but also the interpretation of the translator. A phrase in any language often has nuances and overtones that cannot be expressed in a single phrase in another language. How does one translate the English word "nice" into French or German? How does one translate the Spanish "simpático" into English? In such cases, the translator is forced to choose between the various shades of meaning and opt for the phrase that seems to convey those shades most faithfully.

This is also true of Bible translations. They always reflect, not only the style, but also the biases of the translators. In general, two main approaches have been followed by translators. One has been called the "formal correspondence" approach, and it seeks to translate the biblical text word for word to the point of indicating, by means of different typefaces, when a word had to be added for the sake of clarity or grammar. A typical example of this kind of translation is the King James Version. The second approach, that of "dynamic equivalence," "is concerned first of all with communicating the *content* of the source message in terms meaningful to the receptors. It is thus forced to dispense with *formal* correspondence whenever such correspondence would lead to interference or translationisms that might impede communication."[3] In varying degrees most "contemporary" translations follow this approach, and a good example is the Good News Bible. The choice, however, is not always simple. Take for instance the passage in Luke 13:32, where Jesus refers to Herod as "that fox." What the Greek says is, literally, "fox." Yet, we know that what was meant by calling somebody a "fox" at that time was different from what we mean today when we apply that epithet to someone. Actually, the meaning in Herod's day was closer to what we intend when we call someone a "rat." How, then, should the text be translated? If we say "fox," we are literally correct, but readers will understand something radically different than apparently the evangelist intended. If we follow "dynamic equivalence" to its ultimate consequences and say "rat," we shall be closer to the original import, but we shall be giving the name of an entirely different animal. Obviously, each of these approaches has its shortcomings. Formal correspondence often leads to translations that are hardly intelligible, but dynamic equivalence gives translators greater latitude in which to exercise their biases. Therefore, preachers of liberation must be particularly aware of the manner in which such biases affect various translations, and if at all possible seek a knowledge of the biblical languages which is sufficiently thorough to be able to judge between various possible translations.

It is obviously impossible to review here the biases that appear in various

English translations. But a few examples will give the reader an indication of what some of the problems are.

The use of the words "servant" and "slave" in various English translations of the New Testament would yield ample material for reflection along these lines. For instance, why is it that most translations refer to Paul as a "servant" in Romans 1:1, and to Onesimus as a "slave" in Philemon 16, when in fact the same Greek word is used in both passages? (The main exception is the King James Version, which refers to both Paul and Onesimus as "servants.") Could it not be that, perhaps unconsciously, white translators have been reluctant to have Paul call himself anything as low as a slave? Translators (even the more recent translators of the NRSV) seem to have come to the conclusion that the same word, "doulos," should sometimes be interpreted as "servant" and at other times as "slave," and that they know when to use one word, and when to use the other.

Still dealing with Onesimus and the Epistle to Philemon, we are all well aware of the manner in which that epistle was used in support of slavery, and particularly to argue that runaway slaves ought to be returned to their masters. But what has usually been forgotten is that Paul instructed Philemon to receive Onesimus "no longer as a slave but more than a slave, a beloved brother" (v. 16, NRSV) or "not now as a servant, but above a servant, a brother beloved" (KJV). And, as if to make doubly sure that this was not spiritualized and interpreted in an "inner" sense, so that Onesimus would continue being treated as a slave with the added appellative of "brother," Paul went on to say that this fraternity was to be "both in the flesh and in the Lord" (KJV and NRSV). In spite of this, the traditional interpretation in many circles has been that Paul sent Onesimus back to slavery, with an exhortation to Philemon to call him brother. Thus, the word "slave" was taken literally, and "brother" was taken figuratively, although the text itself gives no basis for such assumptions. Surprisingly, this interpretation became so widespread that it was generally accepted, not only by whites, but also by many African-Americans, with the result that the Epistle to Philemon became rather unpopular in black churches. But what is even more surprising is that the Good News Bible perpetuates that interpretation by obscuring the fact that Paul told Philemon to receive Onesimus "both in the flesh and in the Lord." Compare the import of the following two translations of Philemon 16:

> no longer as a slave but more than a slave, a beloved brother—especially to me but how much more to you, both in the flesh and in the Lord. (NRSV)
> And now he is not just a slave, but much more than a slave: he is a brother in Christ. How much he means to me! And how much more he will mean to you, both as a slave and as a brother in the Lord! (GNB)

The more modern translation, with its effort at dynamic equivalence, has clearly decided that "in the flesh" refers to his slavery, and that Onesimus' brotherhood with Philemon is only "in the Lord"; that is, one is literal, and the other figurative.

Still on the subject of the translation of the Greek term "doulos," it may be significant to note that the NRSV is the first major English translation to translate the well-known Christological hymn in Philippians 2 in the sense that Jesus "took the form of a slave." The King James Version says that Jesus took the form of a "servant." Imagine what the impact would have been if in a slave-holding society the authorized version of Scripture had declared that Jesus "took the form of a slave"!

Another case in point is the choice between "justice" and "righteousness." In the original Greek New Testament, these two are the same word. And yet, by consistently translating that word as "righteousness," many translators have left aside the demands of justice, and texts that may well refer to justice are seen as speaking only of a moral rectitude. Take for instance II Corinthians 6:7, "with the weapons of righteousness for the right hand and for the left"; and 6:14, "For what partnership is there between righteousness and lawlessness?" (NRSV), and substitute the word "justice" for "righteousness." Does that not give the text a biting edge that our more common translations seem to miss?

Still on the question of "justice" and "righteousness," it is significant to note that most modern western European languages have these two options for translating the one Greek word, and that in general those translations done from a position of power—or at least of prestige—seem to prefer "righteousness" and its equivalents, while those done in the midst of persecution, or in other positions of disadvantage, opt for "justice." Again, biblical translation, like biblical interpretation, is not done in a socio-political void.

There are literally hundreds of examples that could be used to show the degree to which sexism has influenced biblical translation. The most common in modern English versions stems from the nature of the English language and its need for an explicit subject for every verb. Since the verbal form "walk" can refer to a number of different subjects (I walk, you walk, we walk, they walk), one cannot simply say "walk," without specifying who does the walking. In this respect, Greek is very different from English, for the subject is included in the verb and does not need to be explicitly stated. (Readers who have not studied Greek, but know the basics of Spanish or Latin, may be helped to understand this usage of Greek verbs by remembering that in both Latin and Spanish "amo" means "I love," and "amas" means "you love.") In the case of the third person, this allows for an indeterminateness that is not possible in English. Take for instance Luke 13:29, where the RSV says: "and men will come from east and west . . . "; the KJV says: "they shall come from the east, and from the west, . . . "; and the NRSV (together with GNB) says: "people will come from east and west . . . " Why is it that one version says "men," another says "they," and still another says "people"?

Because the Greek provides no subject to the verb. It simply uses the third person plural form of the verb, and provides no more determinate subject. Because that cannot be done in English, translators are left with the need to provide a subject. Significantly, both the RSV and J.B. Phillips choose to use "men," thus expressing the commonly held assumption of our society that "man" is the normative form of being human. There are literally dozens of similar cases in which modern translators (particularly J.B. Phillips) have provided the subjects "man," "men," and "he" where the Greek offers none.

Another example that appears throughout is the use of the male plural form to refer to mixed groups. In English, very few words have gender, and those that do usually refer directly to the sex of the person—words such as son, daughter, brother, sister, husband, wife, nephew, niece, etc. Nouns referring to inanimate objects such as chairs and tables have no gender. Certainly articles (the, a, an) and adjectives (good, fast, faithful, etc.) have no gender. Words such as "the" and "dear" do not change, no matter whether one is speaking of "the dear brothers" or "the dear sisters." Thus, if one is speaking about a church in which there are both men and women, one is likely to say, for instance, "the dear Christian brothers and sisters." But one could hardly do this in a language such as Greek (or Latin, Spanish, Italian, or Portuguese) in which not only "brothers" and "sisters" but also "the," "dear," and "Christian" have genders. The result of such an attempt would be a very awkward phrase: the (masc.) dear (masc.) Christian (masc.) brothers and the (fem.) dear (fem.) Christian (fem.) sisters. In order to avoid this awkward repetition, Greek and other languages with similar characteristics make use of the plural masculine form in order to refer to mixed groups. Thus, for instance, in Greek there is a word of "brother" and another for "sister," but when referring to a group of both genders one could easily and normally speak of them as "brothers," thus avoiding the cumbersome repetition of articles, nouns and adjectives.[4] Given the nature of the language, this would not automatically exclude "sisters," as the English would. There is, for instance, a passage in which Herodotus says that among the Pharaohs of Egypt, "brothers"—*adelphoi*—marry each other. Obviously, this cannot be taken literally. It is clear that, in this case at least, "*adelphoi*" means "brothers and sisters" or "siblings."

It is important to understand this, for often the Greek New Testament speaks of *adelphoi*, and we tend to think that the only correct translation is "brothers." To say "brothers and sisters," as the NRSV normally does, would seem to be a concession to modern sensibilities. But that is not the case. Just as the *adelphoi* in the passage from Herodotus does not mean brothers, but siblings of both sexes, so the same word in one of the epistles of Paul may literally and originally mean "brothers and sisters." Such is the nature of the Greek language, even apart from modern considerations regarding inclusive language. And yet, it is interesting to note that until the publication of the NRSV all common English versions of the Bible translate the Greek plural *adelphoi* as "brothers," and never seem even to consider the possibility that this may be a reference to a group which includes both sisters and brothers—in which case the proper and literal translation would be "brothers and sisters." The same is true for other similar cases, such as *huioi*, which may means either "sons" or "sons and daughters."

A very interesting case appears in Romans 16:7. Here two people are called "apostles": Andronicus and Junia (some manuscripts actually say "Julia"). By its form, "Junia" is clearly a feminine name. However, since the two, Andronicus and Junia, are spoken of together, the words for "relatives," "fellow prisoners," and "apostles" are all in the plural masculine form. This does not mean the Junia is a man, for the masculine form would have been used, no matter whether Paul was speaking of two men or of a man and a woman. All that can be said regarding their gender is that we have here two people, and that the name of one of them appears to be feminine, while the other is clearly masculine. And yet, the King James Version takes for granted that both were men, and so translates: "Salute Andronicus and Junia, my kinsmen, and my fellowprisoners, who are of note among the apostles." The RSV carried the matter one step further by calling the two, not only "kinsmen," but also "*men* of great note among the apostles." At this point one wonders whether the translators were led only by grammatical considerations or simply allowed themselves to be influenced by the tacit assumption that no woman could be counted among the apostles. Fortunately, the NRSV offers a more felicitous translation: "Greet Andronicus and Junia, my relatives who were in prison with me; they are prominent among the apostles."

Translations, like all interpretations, have their hidden agendas—sometimes hidden from the translators themselves. Part of the "ideological suspicion" of those who have gone through the hermeneutical circle must be to question every translation and to seek to check it out with the language of origin before deciding that a particular text is as oppressive as we may be told it is. If recourse to the original language is not open to us, we must at least compare several different translations. At this point it may be well to remember that the more a translation relies on the principles of "dynamic equivalence" the more danger there is that the biases of the translators will creep into it.

The dangers and deficiencies of translations that rely on the principle of "dynamic equivalence" are multiplied in the case of paraphrases such as *The Living Bible,* which are worse than useless, for they reflect the cultural biases of the translators at least as much as they reflect the original text. Two examples of how this occurs will suffice. First, in Proverbs 31:18, where the text speaks of a woman who "perceives that her merchandise is profitable," *The Living Bible* says that she "watches for bargains." Secondly, *The Living*

Bible translates the same verb as "preach" when it refers to a man, and as "prophesy" when it refers to a woman (see, for instance, I Cor. 11:4-5). Clearly, what is reflected here is a cultural bias which believes that a woman's proper occupation in the world of economics is to go shopping, and that her proper role in the church does not include preaching.

Lectionaries

Lectionaries are a very useful aid to preaching, for they prevent the preacher from centering on a few favorite passages, books, or themes. All of us have that inclination, and therefore it is helpful to have an outside influence, such as the lectionary, calling our attention to elements in the gospel message which we may have tended to ignore. Widely used lectionaries—such as *The Revised Common Lectionary*[5]—can also remind us that we are part of a greater church, and others are dealing with the same passages at the same time as we are. *The Revised Common Lectionary* is based upon the Roman Catholic lectionary, with significant variations, but it is used by nineteen Protestant denominations, with the exception of Lutherans and Episcopalians.

Lectionaries are also helpful in that sometimes they induce us to face up to the relationship between texts that we would otherwise prefer to keep apart. A case in point is Luke 10:25-42 where the parable of the Good Samaritan and the story of Mary and Martha appear back to back. The common interpretation of the parable is that we ought to be concerned about the physical needs of others, above our religious concerns. But then comes the story of Mary and Martha in which Martha, who is making provision for Jesus' physical needs, is told that Mary has chosen the better part. Our normal inclination is to preach about the Good Samaritan when we feel that the congregation is too engrossed in religious matters and not sufficiently involved in the needs of the world, and to preach on Mary and Martha when we fear that the opposite is true. We get away with this by making sure that there are at least a few months between our sermons on these two texts! But what we are really doing in such cases is manipulating Scripture. *We* know what the two texts say. *We* diagnose the needs of the congregation. *We* prescribe the appropriate text in the appropriate dose. We thus seem to have the same control over the Word of God that a physician has over pills and potions. But a good lectionary can serve as a corrective. In the case of Luke 10, for instance, *The Revised Common Lectionary* makes certain that the Good Samaritan and Mary and Martha are dealt with in the same unbroken continuity which they have in the Gospel of Luke. The lectionary also helps us by prescribing, for the preceding and succeeding Sundays, the setting of Luke in which these passages appear, thus giving an indication the neither the parable nor the episode of Mary and Martha can be correctly understood apart from the inbreaking of the Kingdom, which is the theme of the earlier part of Luke 10.

But in spite of all these values of a lectionary, preachers must not forget that lectionaries are a selection which reflects the prevailing tradition of the church, and that therefore they must be seen with the necessary "ideological suspicion," and corrected accordingly.

The Revised Common Lectionary takes into account a number of criticisms that had been levelled against the previous one. Old Testament texts continue to be chosen most often on the basis of their significance for the Christian religion and its observances, rather than on the basis of their significance in showing God's just and loving dealings with the people. In the revised form of the lectionary, there is an alternate set of selections for part of the year, and in that section the Old Testament selections are chosen independently of the Gospel reading. Even so, although there are many selections from Deuteronomy and Leviticus, not included are the much more radical views of these two books of law, that the land belongs to God and cannot be held in perpetuity by anyone, and that at the time of jubilee there shall be a general release from creditors:

The land shall not be sold in perpetuity, for the land is mine; with me you are but aliens and tenants. Throughout the land that you hold, you shall provide for the redemption of the land.

If anyone of your kin falls into difficulty and sells a piece of property, then the next of kin shall come and redeem what the relative has sold. If the person has no one to redeem it, but then prospers and finds sufficient means to do so, the years since the sale shall be computed and the difference shall be refunded to the person to whom it was sold, and the property shall be returned. But if there is not sufficient means to recover it, what was sold shall remain with the purchaser until the year of jubilee; in the jubilee it shall be released, and the property shall be returned (Lev. 25:23-28, NRSV).

Though several passages from Proverbs are chosen, Proverbs 30:7-9, which could be very important in a consumer society, is not used. It reads:

Two things I ask of you;
> do not deny them to me before I die;
Remove far from me falsehood and lying;
> give me neither poverty nor riches;
> feed me with the food that I need,
or I shall be full, and deny you,
> and say, "Who is the Lord?"
or I shall be poor, and steal,
> and profane the name of my God.

There is another possible omission that is very significant. The account of the escape from Egypt, which liberation theologians see as the great instance of God's saving action in the Old Testament, is listed for the Easter Eve Vigil. The Easter Vigil is an excellent place for it, because it shows the connection between the escape from Egypt and redemption through the resurrection of Jesus. But there is no such vigil in many Protestant churches. In adapting a lectionary to their own uses, many Protestant congregations would simply eliminate those texts, because the lack of awareness of the issues of liberation make it possible for them to leave out this crucial saving act of God. Should it not be moved to Easter Day in those circumstances!

An interesting example of cropping has to do with the slaughter of the innocents. *The Revised Common Lectionary* sets as the Gospel lesson for the first Sunday after Christmas, Matthew 2:13-23. The historical reason why this text appears in this place is that the church has traditionally celebrated the day of the Holy Innocents on December 28, and therefore the readings having to do with the slaughter of the infants and the flight into Egypt were placed around that date. But this breaks the sequence of the Gospel narrative, for it places the lessons having to do with the arrival of the magi on January 6, long after both the slaughter of the children and the flight into Egypt. Were that the real sequence, the magi would have found an empty stable!

When we apply our ideologically suspicious methodology to all this, we discover that the present order of readings breaks the connection between the action of the magi and their consequences. The Gospel text, read in sequence, shows that both the slaughter of the innocents and the flight into Egypt are the direct result of the magi's actions. But the magi have become objects of veneration in the church. As signs of the coming of the Gospel to the Gentiles, they are our forerunners. In popular tradition, they are rich and wise men (the word *magus* does not necessarily mean a "wise" person, as we understand wisdom today, but rather an astrologer, diviner, and interpreter of dreams). We even take them to be kings, although again, there is nothing in the text that says they were. Such powerful, rich, and wise men cannot make the stupid blunder of warning Herod about the birth of Jesus, and thus causing the flight into Egypt and the slaughter of the innocents. Therefore, the church calendar, and the lectionaries based on it, hide the fact that they did—although some older Protestant liturgies did have the readings sequentially correct, because they did not celebrate Holy Innocents. And yet, this blunder of the supposedly wise and religious, hidden by the wise and religious who have developed the church year, is crystal clear to the poor in Nicaragua, as we shall see later.

The lectionary assumes that the lessons will be read in services that do not necessarily include preaching, and therefore might well not be discussed. Probably for this reason some passages that might well present problems if they were read without further comment are omitted. A chief example of this is the total elimination in this *Revised Common Lectionary* of any of the household legislation that discusses the duties of wives and husbands, children and fathers, slaves and masters. It is probably very wise to omit these in such a lectionary, but then it means that a preacher who follows the lectionary may well never deal with some of the very difficult texts that really need to be considered. We will deal later with these particular passages.

In conclusion, lectionaries, being a part of the tradition of the church, reflect that tradition, in both its positive and its negative features. Therefore, the preacher's attitude toward them should be the same as toward Christian tradition in general. We accept them as part of the continuing history of which we also are a part. We value what they have to teach us regarding the amplitude of the biblical message. Yet we do not submit to them blindly, but rather approach them with the same "ideological suspicion" with which we approach the entirety of Christian tradition and theology.

Commentaries

Nor are commentaries ideologically neutral. Most of them take for granted that the best and only way to understand the Bible is through meticulous and scholarly study of words, historical data, redaction, forms, etc. Some of the most widely used commentaries limit themselves to this sort of historical, critical and philological inquiry. In this sense, the *International Critical Commentary*, which began publication a century ago, is very similar to *The Anchor Bible* and other contemporary counterparts. They take for granted that the task of the commentator is to respond to questions such as the sources which a biblical author or redactor employed, the process through which a book attained its present form, and at best the original message of the book for its first intended readers. That the biblical text is being read today as authoritative by a community of faith does not seem to be a significant factor for such commentators.

A leading biblical scholar has pointed out that the supposedly objective methods of historical criticism have their own agenda:

The methods in which we have been schooled inevitably operate with hidden criteria (modern rationalism) that decide beforehand what would be included in a text. This method has devised respectable strategies for disposing of what is unacceptable to the modern consciousness, so that issues of artistry that constitute new reality have been handled either by dismissive labels of literary genre or by source divisions that divide and conquer ironies and contradictions in the text. The outcome of historical criticism is most often to provide a text that is palatable to modern rationality, but that in the process has been emptied of much that is most interesting, most poignant, and most "disclosing" in the text.[6]

On the other hand, and particularly in the more conservative sectors of the church, a number of commentaries circulate which are clearly intended for the pulpit or for private devotion, and which tend to disregard the sort of historical questions which seem to be paramount for the more scholarly commentaries.

The Interpreter's Bible, probably the most widely used commentary among mainline Protestant preachers, combines the defects of both sorts of commentary. For each book of the Bible, the exegetical commentary was written by an author, and the exposition by another author who often did not take the exegesis into account. The impression given may be a true reflection of the sad state of mainline Protestant biblical studies and preaching: there seems to be an inadequate relation between the two. This is in stark contrast to the commentaries of John Calvin in the sixteenth century, which combine the best scholarship available at the time with a strong sense that the commentary is intended to relate the ancient text to the contemporary community of faith.

More recently, other commentaries have sought to bridge this gap. Some of the earlier ones were not commentaries on entire books, but rather commentaries on the lectionary. A number of these tried to expound biblical texts for today while taking seriously the results of biblical scholarship. A number of liberation theologians have written commentaries on individual books of the Bible in which they make use of generally accepted biblical scholarship while relating the message of the text to the struggles in which they are involved. *The Women's Bible Commentary*[7] is a one-volume commentary written by women, paying special attention to texts and issues that are particularly relevant to women. Beginning in 1990, a group of Latin American and Hispanic American scholars began production of the *Comentario Bíblico Hispanoamericano,* a fifty volume series which seeks to study the text both in its original setting and composition and as it functions in the community today. The forthcoming *New Interpreter's Bible* promises to be an improvement on its former counterpart by assigning the exegetical and homiletical interpretations of each text to a single author. It also intends to take into account the contributions and perspectives of women and ethnic minorities .

Still, most of these commentaries take for granted that those who have critical, historical and philological tools are at an advantage when it comes to interpreting the Bible. At a certain level, that is obviously true. On the other hand, it is necessary to insist that no amount of scholarship ever suffices to unlock a text that deals with things that have been hidden from the wise and the learned and revealed to babes.

At this point many will agree, and insist that true understanding also requires piety, that it is impossible to understand the biblical message as an outsider, as someone who is not committed to it. And that is precisely the point. But we must hasten to add that such piety, which is absolutely necessary to understand the Bible, must be *biblical* piety. It cannot be what our culture, and many of our churches after it, deem to be piety. It must be that piety which consists in being part of the people of God, marching after the promised Reign of peace and justice. In other words, it must be piety which lives in symbiosis with what liberation theologians call "praxis."

The Bible was written in a pre-Enlightenment period. Those of us who approach it with a post-Enlightenment mentality may thereby gain some insight into it. But in another way, the poor and uneducated, many of whom still live and read as before the Enlightenment, may have access to deeper insights that simply are not directly available to the scholar. If the message of the Bible is "good news to the poor," it follows that the poor are at a decided advantage when it comes to understanding it. Furthermore, there is always the danger that commentaries and expositions written by the non-poor may obscure rather than illumine significant elements in the text.

This does not mean that the preacher should not use commentaries. Without them, we could easily miss the meaning of many words, the grammatical structure of passages, parallel texts that illumine their meaning, historical situations that shaped the passage, etc. But it does mean that we should approach biblical commentaries, no matter how seemingly objective, with the same ideological suspicion with which we approach the entirety of Christian tradition and theology.

As a normal practice, it may be well to postpone the reading of commentaries until, through the use of some of the methods outlined in this book, we come to the point where we hear what we believe to be God's Word in the text for our concrete situation and struggle. After that, commentaries will prove useful instruments whereby to make certain that we have not completely misinterpreted the text, or to discover nuances and connections which we had not noticed before.

III

The Neglected
Interpreters

In the previous chapter, we gave some examples of the difficulties that stand in the way of our listening anew to the biblical text. Most of these are hidden and therefore difficult to overcome. The present chapter and the next will give some examples of the ways in which a preacher can seek to hear the word of the Bible in a new and liberating way.

The End of the Lone-Ranger Bible Study

For too long there has been in Protestant circles an excessive emphasis on private Bible study. There is no doubt that such study is necessary. It does not take ten people working together to look up a word in a Hebrew lexicon. When one adds to this the devotional dimension, there is also no doubt that there is an important place in the Christian life for private devotions, and that these ought to be centered on the study of the Bible. But the problem comes when we seem to say that private Bible study is somehow better or deeper or more meaningful than corporate study—when we forget that the Bible comes out of a community and is addressed to a community. As a result of this individualistic approach to the Bible, there are some in our culture for whom private reading of Scripture and prayer are the ultimate forms of Christian worship, and for whom, therefore, the church is a dispensable item. One does not need the community of faith for the reading or understanding of Scripture. One's own interpretation is quite sufficient. Radio and TV religious programs give an illusion of community, but actually increase the individualism of the listener, who tunes in or out readily.

Individualism has become an even more serious problem for English readers due to the manner in which English grammar has evolved. In modern English, there is no difference between the singular "you" and the plural "you." This creates problems even in everyday conversation. We who write this book have repeatedly had experiences in which this dual use of the word "you" has led to confusion. Someone calls us from California, and speaking to one of us says, "we want to invite you to come and deliver a series of lectures." Somehow, the one who answers must prolong the conversation until they find out, without asking too bluntly, if "you" means "me" or "us."

In fact in very few portions of Scripture is the reader addressed as "you" in the singular. One clear case is the Epistle to Philemon. Two other cases are the dedication to Theophilus in Luke–Acts and Timothy and Titus in the Pastoral Epistles. But in both of these cases the singular "you" is understood by most scholars as a literary device to address a much wider, and plural, audience. And, even in these cases, as in the rest of Scripture, what gave them authority as part of the canon was not their private reading, but their reading in the setting of worship.

The impact of a purely individualistic reading of Scripture goes far beyond what immediately comes to mind—a loss of the sense of being a community. It also obscures from us some of the dimensions of what Scripture may be saying. Take for instance the very much debated passages in Ephesians and elsewhere about wives and husbands, masters and slaves. The early church was a very mixed group. It is one thing for this to be read out loud to a mixed group in the early church, where the husbands and the masters receive their share of very sobering instruction which the wives and the slaves are privileged to overhear, and quite another for a woman today to read it in private trying to determine how a good wife ought to behave. The author of Ephesians intended for the wives to overhear the word addressed to their husbands, "be subject to one another out of reverence for Christ," "husbands should love their wives as their own bodies"; and for slaves to overhear the masters being addressed: "masters, do the same to them, and forbear threatening." Granted, such public reading does not solve all the problems posed by these passages; but purely private reading does exacerbate the problems.

Scripture is addressed to a community, and to individuals as part of that gathering. Even read privately, there is the need to see that the Word comes to us as those who are called to or are already part of the People of God. Scripture itself often calls the community of faith to remember their ancestors—either their sinfulness so that the current People would not be so tempted, or their faith which should be continued. But that is not the way it is usually read in our culture. Even the way we tell Bible stories to our children shows a strong individualistic bias. We have the heroes who are to be models, but the stories about the community of faith may be ignored, even when the hero would not have been understood individualistically by the writers or the hearers of Scripture in past centuries.

Things were very different in the early church. The printing press was yet to appear, so copies of Scripture were not available for all to have at home, and therefore when the congregation gathered, a great deal of time was spent reading the Scripture—at first the Old Testament, to which soon were added the "memoirs of the apostles" (Gospels) and the Epistles. The sermon was expected to be an exposition of Scripture. Lay people learned many passages by heart and had a sense that they knew and understood what the Bible was saying. They listened to the readings eagerly, even coming early to the worship services so that they could hear more Scripture read aloud before the service began.

It may be argued that the invention of the printing press, and the resultant fact that Christians can read their Bibles at home, has changed this situation, and that therefore there is little or no need for that sort of corporate Bible study. But the problem is that most of the Bible was written to be read, not in private, but in public, often within the context of corporate worship. Just as it is not the same to read a sermon as it is to hear it preached, it is not the same to read the Bible in private as it is to read and hear it being read in the midst of the People of God. The Lone-Ranger student of the Bible loses a great deal that cannot be regained by any amount of study or private devotion.

To make matters worse, in the services of some of our churches—often those that pride themselves on being most "biblical"—very little attention is paid to the Bible. In some cases, even the sermon, rather than attempting to put us under the scrutiny and the mercy of the Word of God, uses the biblical text as a pretext, as a jumping off point from which to go far afield.

Unfortunately, there are too many examples of this kind of preaching. Yet, we have encountered none worse than a sermon we heard a few years ago. The text was from the book of Revelation: "And the sea was no more." "Why will the sea be no more?" asked the preacher. "Because in the sea there are monsters. There are sharks, like Jaws. . . . But the worst of all the monsters of the sea is the octopus. The octopus has eight tentacles, and it grabs you, and it squeezes you, and it crushes you. And so is the octopus of sin. It too has eight tentacles. First, there is the tentacle of pride. . . . Then there is the tentacle of lust." And so he went, on and on, finally to come to his conclusion: "Therefore, let us come out of the tentacles of the octopus of sin and into the arms of Jesus!"

The obvious shortcoming of this sort of preaching is that it ultimately ignores or circumvents the authority of Scripture, which is made to say whatever the preacher wishes. But a further, and often unrecognized, consequence of this proceeding is that people are discouraged from the study of Scripture. Even if they are enlightened and strengthened in their Christian lives by such a sermon, they see no way that they could have learned from the biblical text what the preacher claims to find in it. Rather than encouraging their hearers to delve further into the Bible, such preachers actually are discouraging them. The Bible becomes an esoteric book that only those with specialized education or gifts can possibly be able to understand. It is not a book for the lay Christian, but only for the "professional." This is hardly an attitude that should be encouraged in the church.

But the Lone Ranger himself did not roam the West alone. He had Tonto with him. Tonto, whose name means "dimwit," as any Hispanic in the Southwest would know. Tonto, who hardly ever spoke, except for an occasional, either enigmatic or meaningless "kemo sabe." And in spite of this the white hero was called "lone," because his Indian companion, who repeatedly saved his life, simply did not count. He did not count for two reasons: first, he was seen as a projection of his white leader; second, the Lone Ranger never seemed to take the time to listen to him.

There is then a type of "Lone-Ranger" Bible study which, although not necessarily done in private, is done in the same sort of almost meaningless company which Tonto provided for the hero. This happens when our biblical interpretation fails to be challenged by others, either because they share our own perspective, or because, since they differ from us, we classify them as "Tontos" whose perspectives we need not take into account.

The ideologically suspicious preacher soon comes to the realization that, given the social structure of our denominations and of our housing patterns, it is very difficult to avoid the Lone-Ranger Bible study. We may try to have more corporate study of the Bible, and certainly something is gained from doing so; but it is still difficult to provide for the various perspectives which would allow us to see the Bible in a different light.

Even within the social uniformity and racial monochrome of most of our churches, a degree of diversity could be helpful. People of different ages and genders, for instance, are present. And yet, even here church leaders segregate our Bible study by age and by gender! Of course we expect a place for a graded Sunday school and for women's circles of Bible study, but do we not lose something of the enrichment that we could be to each other when most or all our study of the Bible is done in such settings? If it is true that God has "hidden these things from the wise and understanding and revealed them to babes" (Luke 10:21), do not adults cheat themselves out of the opportunity for deeper insight into the will of God when they fail to provide for Bible study that cuts across age groups? And, if it is true that those who are oppressed and whom society counts as nothing go first into the Reign of God, do not young adults miss an opportunity to see the work of God when they put the aged "out to pasture" and do not give them an opportunity to show them, through constant interaction in love, what the

Bible says from the perspective of those who once were powerful and respected, but now often find themselves merely tolerated?

Something similar is true in the case of women. The difference between their experience and that of men should be a significant factor in the study of the Bible, especially since traditionally most biblical commentary and exegesis has been done from a male perspective. It is common for male preachers to try to guess what women will find significant, or how they will react to a certain text. And usually they fail miserably! An easy experiment, which may serve to show this, is to ask a group of men to list the five passages in the Bible that they believe will be most significant for women, and then to ask a group of women to list the five passages that they themselves have found most significant in their Christian lives. Chances are that there will be very little overlapping between the two lists. Men will usually choose those passages that speak about women, whereas women will list those that speak of strength in the midst of difficulty or of confidence when there is cause for despair. What this shows is that, quite unconsciously, men tend to believe that the Bible is addressed to them, for they are the typical, normative human beings, and that only those passages which speak of females will be of significance to women. It often comes as a shock to discover, not only that these are not the passages that the women list, but also that their interpretations of the passages that they do choose show valuable insights derived from their experience as females.

When it comes to questions of class, race, and culture, the average North American white church finds it much more difficult to overcome the Lone-Ranger syndrome. Many members of our congregations are willing to see their sisters and brothers of other groups as fellow travelers in the Christian life, and are even willing to help them along. But they still will tend to see them as "Tontos" whose contribution to the understanding of the Christian message will be no more than a grunt or an occasional "kemo sabe." Even where there is an interest in hearing what these people have to say, the social and racial composition of most white churches makes it very difficult. In order to be able to listen to what the supposed "Tontos" are saying and to the way they experience and interpret the message of the Bible, it is necessary to have a close association with them, to share in their experience, in a way and to a degree that very few in the white community are willing to risk.

What then of the sincere, white, male preacher who believes that there are valuable insights in these communities and wishes to pursue them to make them his own and to lead his congregation in hearing them? For such a person, there is only one way: the pain and struggle of the hermeneutic circle. He cannot live out of another's experience of oppression. He must discover how the system that oppresses the African American, the Hispanic, the native American, and the woman, also oppresses him. He must come to see for himself how much of the theology he has been taught serves to bolster that system of oppression. He must develop the ideological suspicion without which there is no liberating theology. He must begin to work for his own emancipation, and do his theology out of that struggle. And then he will really be able to look at the theology of other groups, and to learn from it.

Once the preacher comes to this point, there are a number of resources available. These are helpful, both for the white male preacher who must do groundwork on the meaning of his own situation, and for those preachers who belong to other groups, but who may gain insight from the understandings of others in similar settings. In the next two sections of this chapter, we shall deal with some of those resources.

Resources from Christian Tradition

It may seem odd to begin a discussion on a liberating reading of Scripture and of theology by speaking of the resources of Christian tradition. Indeed, many of those who are involved in various struggles for liberation feel that Christian tradition has been so oppressive that it must be discarded altogether. Others, mostly those who come out of a background of liberal theology, have been taught that the past is a burden of which they must rid themselves, and that what must be done is to interpret Christianity in a "modern" way, more adapted to our present circumstances.

It is true that a great deal of Christian tradition has been oppressive. It is also true that, if the Word of God is to be relevant, it must be relevant **today**, and that the very notion of history, so central to the gospel itself, implies that today's preaching will not be the same as yesterday's. In fact, preaching would not be necessary if there were no need to relate the gospel message to a contemporary situation. In spite of all of this, there is still a great deal of Christian tradition that must be recovered.

That recovery is a difficult task, for from a very early date the process began by which those elements of the tradition that could not be assimilated into the status quo were suppressed or ignored. We have already referred to Eusebius' attempt to show that the persecutions were little more than a grave misunderstanding on the part of the Roman Empire. More recent historians have also read history in a similar manner. For instance, treatises on the ethics of the early church deal almost exclusively with sexual mores, lying, homicide, and so forth, but fail to take into account the astonishing teachings of early Christian writers regarding property, the use and distribution of wealth, and the like. The reason for this is that the definition of what are "ethical" questions has been narrowed in our capitalist society, precisely so as not to include issues such as whether private property is morally correct, or what are the rights of the poor. On the basis of such a definition,

52

historians of Christian ethics tend to ignore the very radical things that have been said in earlier centuries of Christian history, and thus give us the impression that today's radical questioning of the rights of property, for instance, is a new phenomenon, about which Christian tradition has little to say.

The ideologically suspicious preacher is not quick to accept such a verdict, but rather asks a further question: Is the history of Christian ethics a faithful rendering of what ancient Christians actually taught, or is it rather one more case in which the interests of the powerful are being served by what seems to be impartial scholarship? Even before examining the evidence, such an ideologically suspicious person will remember that the early church was not generally composed of rich and powerful people, and will therefore expect to find a different perspective than that which seems to pervade Christian teaching in later times.

Although this is not the only issue of concern to liberation theologies, let us for the moment center our attention on economic matters, and we may be surprised by what we shall find in early Christian writing. On this score, the picture that most of us have is that of a primitive church that had all things in common, discovered that such a system did not work, and promptly forgot it, together with any attempt to reorder or critique the existing economic system. But, although it is true that soon the church began having some rich folk in its midst, and therefore began to mollify some of Jesus' strictures against the rich, it is also true that for centuries it kept alive an understanding of God's will that there should be neither rich nor needy, but that all should have that which was necessary for their sustenance, and that some of its leaders had very harsh words to say about the prevailing economic system and those who profited from it.

Ignatius of Antioch, who wrote seven letters early in the second century while on his way to martyrdom, has been correctly depicted as a zealous defender of orthodoxy. But what most scholars have failed to note is that to him orthodoxy was not only a matter of proper doctrine, but also a matter of right relationship to those in need:

> As to those who profess teachings that have nothing to do with the grace of Jesus Christ . . . you must come to a full realization that those doctrines are completely opposed to the mind of God, for they care nothing about love, they care not for the widow and the orphan, they care not for the hard pressed, nor do they care who is in chains or free, or who is hungry or thirsty.[1]

And a few decades later, Hermas wrote that those who are in need live anxious and tormented lives to the point that some of them are driven to commit homicide, and therefore any Christian who knows of a person in dire need and fails to respond to that situation may be guilty of homicide.[2]

53

On the other hand, already at the time of Hermas, the rich were joining the church in increasing numbers, and there were those who sought to make it easier for them. Thus, for instance, Clement of Alexandria, in his treatise, *Who Is the Rich to Be Saved?* turned what Jesus had to say to the rich ruler into an allegory and said that what mattered was not the riches themselves, but one's attachment to them. If one had riches, but one loved God above them, they would be no obstacle to salvation, but rather a help, for one could then perform greater works of charity.

The question of property and its use, however, became crucial after the conversion of Constantine. Many who flocked to the church were rich. Most church leaders simply accepted such people and were all too glad to have them add part of their wealth and prestige to the church. But there were many others who, while not absolutely refusing to receive the rich, felt that they must insist on the old Christian teachings regarding riches and the responsibility of those who had more than they needed toward those others who were in want. Most of the great "fathers" of the church held economic views which would be considered quite radical in our day.

Ambrose of Milan, for instance, says that "the earth has been created in common for all, rich and poor. Why do you [the rich] claim for yourselves the right to own the land?"[3] And in another place he says that "God created all things to be the common food, and the land to be the common possession of all. Thus, nature begat the common right, and usurpation begat the private."[4] The result of this is that, when you give to the needy, "you do not give to the poor what is yours, but rather return what is theirs."[5] The reason why the birds of the air do not go hungry is that they do not claim anything in particular for each of them, but rather share equally the bounty of God.[6] But a few rich claim everything for themselves, "not only the land, but the sky, the air, the sea,"[7]—and here one is reminded of today's quip that solar energy will be developed when someone invents a way to hang a meter on the sun—with the result that "every day are the needy murdered."[8]

These views were shared by many of the great Christian leaders of the fourth and fifth centuries. Among them, Basil the Great says to the rich: "The bread that you hoard belongs to the hungry. The cloak that you keep in your chests belongs to the naked. The shoes that rot in your house belong to the unshod."[9] And therefore, anyone who can do something for the needy and refuses to do so is justly condemned as a homicide.[10] But Basil goes even farther than Ambrose in attacking the wanton growth of capital: "The beasts become fertile when they are young, but quickly cease to be so. But capital produces interest from the very beginning, and this in turn multiplies unto infinity. All that grows ceases to do so when it reaches its normal size. But the money of the greedy never stops growing."[11] And this progression of power is ever accelerating:

> Those who attain a certain level of power use those whom they have already enslaved in order to gain more strength to commit ever greater iniquities,

and by using them they enslave those who were still free. Then their greater power becomes a new weapon for evil. And as a result those whom they first injured now have no other option but to help them, and thus collaborate in the evil and iniquity committed against the others.[12]

A host of other witnesses could be adduced to show the radical economic doctrine of those great church leaders. Jerome agrees with the common saying that those who are rich are such either through their own injustice or through that of those whose property they have inherited.[13] Zeno of Verona says that greed is the reason why some people's granaries are full, while others' stomachs are empty. And he goes on to comment that, whereas that which has been taken by force can sometimes be recovered, that which has been taken under the shade of the law can never be recovered.[14] Augustine,[15] Lactantius,[16] Cyril,[17] and Gregory the Great[18] are all in agreement that private property is not of God, but is rather the reason why many are in want, and also the root of discord and war.

Because this is a book on preaching, we now turn to the sermons of the most renowned of the preachers of antiquity, St. John Chrysostom—"the goldenmouthed." Following the long established tradition to which we have already referred, Chrysostom agrees that iniquity is the only possible source of great riches, for if it is not the very person who is opulent that has committed the necessary iniquities, it must have been that person's ancestors.[19] Since the earth is the Lord's, and the fullness thereof, nothing is to be held by any as privately owned.[20] The rich are not really such, for what they have belongs to others.[21] Anything that one might have, even though legitimately earned, in truth belongs to the poor.[22] And the unjust distribution of wealth increases as time goes by, for all are drawn into the whirlwind of greed, with each trying to outdo those who have gone on before.[23] The rich try to glorify themselves by building opulent palaces, but after their death passersby who never knew them say, "How many tears must that house have cost! How many widows must have suffered injustice, and laborers cheated out of their wages!"[24] Therefore, the result of the vain glory of the rich is exactly the opposite of what they had sought, for even after their death they are cursed, and even by those who never knew them. Finally, it is significant that, commenting on Matthew 25, Chrysostom points out that the judge does not condemn those on his left "because you fornicated, because you committed adultery, because you stole, because you gave false witness or committed perjury. All of these sins are obviously evil, but not as great as callousness and lack of humanity."[25]

Such were the teachings of the first centuries regarding property, riches, and the economic order. And although never again as prevalent as at that time, such teachings were never entirely abandoned.[26]

So far we have dealt only with the question of riches and of the existing economic order. But it is well known that, on such matters as slavery, the church remained silent for centuries. At least, so have we been led to believe. However, when we begin studying the tradition on our own, without the filtering process that has become so common, we find startling cases of opposition to slavery, such as the following words of Gregory of Nyssa, addressed to a slaveowner:

> "I have bought slaves, male and female." Pray tell, at what price? What have you found among all the creatures that is worth as much as human nature? How much money is the mind worth? How many staters did you pay in order to walk away with this creature of God? "Let us make man in our own image and likeness," said God. Tell me, then, who dares buy, who dares sell, one who is the image of God, who is to rule over the earth, who received from God as an heir all that there is upon the earth? Such power belongs only to God. And I am inclined to say that not even to God.[27]

And yet, we were told that it took Christians centuries to come to the conclusion that slavery was against the divine will, when what in fact did happen was that voices such as that of Gregory and Chrysostom were drowned by those in the church who catered to the powerful.

Surely when it comes to the issues of women and their place in society the situation must be different. And indeed it is, for most of the writings that we have come from males—many of them male ascetics who felt threatened by the very existence of women. But even in this case one occasionally finds surprising words, such as the following, addressed by Cyprian to a consecrated virgin in the church:

> "I will multiply," says God to the woman, "thy sorrows and thy groanings, and in sorrow shalt thou bring forth children, and thy desire shall be to thy husband, and he shall rule over thee." You are free from this sentence. You do not fear the sorrows and the groans of women. You have no fear of child-bearing; nor is your husband lord over you; but your Lord and Head is Christ, after the likeness and in place of man; with that of men your lot and your condition is equal.[28]

Ecology is a very modern concern, and we might imagine that the early church had little to say about that. Indeed, the term would not appear in an index of patristic literature. However, many in the early period tended to see God's redemptive activity as cosmic in scope, rather than dealing only with human beings. Therefore there is much to be said about God's concern for the future of non-human creation. There is an "earthiness" about redemption that later centuries would lose. For instance, Irenaeus includes far more than individual human beings in God's plan for salvation. In discussing Isaiah 11:6-9—the "peaceable kingdom" passage—Irenaeus opposes an allegorical interpretation of the animals and writes:

> I am quite aware that some persons endeavour to refer these words to the case of savage men, both of different nations and various habits, who come to believe, and when they have believed, act in harmony with the righteous.

But although this is [true] now with regard to some men coming from various nations to the harmony of the faith, nevertheless in the resurrection of the just [the words shall also apply] to those animals mentioned. For God is rich in all things. And it is right that when the creation is restored, all the animals should obey and be in subjection to man, and revert to the food originally given by God (for they had been originally subjected in obedience to Adam), that is, the productions of the earth. But some other occasion, and not the present, is [to be sought] for showing that the lion shall [then] feed on straw. And this indicates the large size and rich quality of the fruits. For if that animal, the lion, feeds upon straw [at that period], of what a quality must the wheat itself be whose straw shall serve as suitable food for lions?[29]

In conclusion, although there is no doubt that a great deal of Christian tradition has been oppressive, it is also true that there has been a filtering of the tradition, a selective forgetfulness, so that what we now perceive is a distorted view of the past of the church. Thus, the preacher will carry the principle of ideological suspicion a step further and refuse to take truisms for granted when we are told that there is nothing useful in the church's past. It may well be that the seemingly sympathetic statement is simply an expression of the way tradition appears after it has been filtered by the interests of the powerful. It may well be that a rereading of documents from the Christian past, particularly those produced by people who were persecuted, maligned, or otherwise opposed by the powerful, will yield fresh insights into the meaning of Scripture when read, so to speak, "from below." We need to remember that early monasticism was a protest against the way the church changed once it became dominated by the concerns of the powerful. Therefore, theology written by those who have taken vows of voluntary poverty often reflect the views of the poor. Ambrose, Augustine, Basil the Great, Gregory the Great, and many of the others quoted above were part of that company, as well as bishops in the church. Their writings can be very rewarding. As a more immediate measure, whenever one is working with a specific biblical text it can also be helpful to check the Scripture reference index that is usually included in the standard translations of these works.

Contemporary Resources

In order to avoid the Lone-Ranger syndrome, the preacher may begin to establish a dialogue with earlier Christian tradition. But this is a life-long task, and cannot replace the face-to-face contact with living dialogue partners. There can be study groups set up within a ministerial alliance in a local community—or simply by neighboring pastors. This is particularly useful where pastors use *The Revised Common Lectionary*. Then the study can focus on the preaching for a specific day. Because this lectionary is used with adaptation by many denominations, including Protestants and Catholics, such study can challenge the different traditional interpretations we all bring to a text.

The past several years have seen many more minorities and women in this country publish commentaries—including lectionary commentaries—as well as sermons. In addition, there is increasing availability of such resources from around the world—from Asia and Africa, from Latin America and Eastern Europe. Each of these can be very helpful.

African-Americans, Hispanics, women, and others who already know and study the writings of representatives of their own groups do not need to be encouraged to do so, for the major figures will already be familiar and helpful to them. However, all may need to be encouraged to read the writings of other groups, as well as interpretations coming from the Third World. This is important, for these various groups will necessarily clash. African-Americans resent white women, Hispanics or Asian-Americans entering the labor market and taking the lower paying jobs that previously were theirs. African Americans understandably might resent the growing attention which the Hispanic and Asian minorities are receiving in the media. All oppressed groups in the United States will find their situation worsened by any international economic changes that lessens the flow of wealth to the United States. Furthermore, those who are in power will foster such conflicts between various oppressed groups, so that the conflict is deflected from their communities. The result is a tendency for each group to look after itself—and in a certain way they must, for no one else will.

In particular, English-speaking persons must be very careful in not imposing on other languages English solutions regarding gender. Most languages reflect the culture which gave them shape; and, since such cultures are often sexist, languages also tend to be sexist. Yet, they do this in different ways, and therefore solutions that work in one language do not work in another. Much significant work has been done in English, in order to find ways to make the language more inclusive in terms of gender. It is necessary for those who speak other languages to work in the same direction with reference to their own languages. However, when English-speakers seek to impose on those other languages solutions that work in English, they often project an imperialistic attitude, and a lack of sensitivity to the structure of languages, that is justly resented by others.[30]

In order to minimize such clashes, we must remember that we are not struggling only against a particular person or group that oppresses us. We are struggling against systems that prevent the fulfillment of God's purposes for all creation. There is a connection between racism, classism, colonialism, and sexism. Each of our groups may be attacking the apocalyptic beast from a different angle, and the beast may defend itself by setting us against each other. But we know that the beast is only one, and that the victory won by the Lamb and promised to us is also one.

For these reasons, preachers who are related to one group ought not eschew those resources which reflect other backgrounds. From these they will come to a deeper understanding of the nature of the oppression against which we must all struggle, and will also gain insight into the meaning of the gospel message which they could not have gained from their own group.

Furthermore, as has already been pointed out, we stand at more than one place in the oppressor-oppressed continuum. An Hispanic male may be part of the oppressed minority, but as a male he must also become aware of the oppression of women, both in his culture and in others. A white North American woman may well be aware of the difficulties of her own situation, but from the point of view of those in poor countries, she is part of the society of over-consumption which so oppresses the Third World. In addition, women of every racial and national group need to encounter the views of other women—and there are now writings in translation that make that possible for English-speaking readers. Therefore, as each of us approaches the resources available from other groups, we must use our own hermeneutical circle to understand what these resources have to say.

Obviously, we cannot offer here an exhaustive introduction to all such resources. We shall attempt simply to offer some examples, to show what words of biblical and theological insight are coming from those whom the Lone Rangers take to be no more than dimwitted Tontos.

Unfortunately, the insights of the poor seldom reach printed form directly. We have a starling exception in Ernesto Cardenal's *The Gospel in Solentiname*.[31] Cardenal is a mystic and a poet, a priest and a political activist, who founded the lay monastery of Our Lady of Solentiname on an island in a lake in Nicaragua. This was during the time of Somoza, before the Sandinistas came to power. In fact, after the events that we are describing here, but still during the war that led to the downfall of Somoza, the settlement was attacked by the military, and many were killed.

On Sundays, after the reading of the Gospel, Cardenal encouraged the people of the islands—mostly fishermen and their wives, with an occasional student back home for the weekend—to discuss the gospel lesson for the day. The book is simply the transcribed tapes of those conversations. The North American reader may be surprised—perhaps even shocked—by the radical political views of the group and by the way these views are related to the gospel. This alone may serve as a corrective to our tendency to read the Bible in purely "religious" terms. But there is also in the comments of many of these uneducated people an insight into the meaning of various texts, an ability to see what scholarly commentators hardly ever note, which seems to prove the contention that the poor and the oppressed have an edge when it comes to understanding the meaning of the Bible.

In discussing the Annunciation, for instance (Luke 1:26-36), these poor people seem to be much more aware of what is going on than are most of our better educated congregations:

> Someone said: "That angel was being subversive just by announcing that. It's as though someone in Somoza's Nicaragua was announcing a liberator " . . . And another added: "And Mary joins the ranks of the subversives, too, just by receiving that message. I suppose that by doing that she probably felt herself entering into a kind of underground. The birth of the liberator had to be kept secret. It would be known only by the most trusted and a few of the poor people around there, villagers."[32]

And at the end of the conversation a certain Alejandro shows a profound understanding of the relationship between obedience, love, and risk: "It seems to me that here we should admire above all her [Mary's] obedience. And so we should be ready to obey too. This obedience is revolutionary, because it's obedience to love. Obedience to love is very revolutionary, because it commands us to disobey everything else."[33]

There may be much here that an average North American reader will find strange, and even offensive. Yet, the insight remains valuable, that what is taking place in the Annunciation is very risky business. Mary is not risking only her good name, as those of us who have been brought up in a middle-class mores will readily understand. She is also risking her very life, by consenting to bear a child who will challenge the existing order.

Let us look at another example from the same book. We have already referred to the political blunder of the magi as they asked around in Jerusalem where was the new king of the Jews that had been born. This point, usually missed by commentators, did not escape the sagacity of these poor and uneducated Nicaraguans, and one of them remarked that "it would be like someone going to Somoza now to ask him where's the man who's going to liberate Nicaragua."[34]

A final example comes from a discussion of the Wedding at Cana (John 2:1-12). We are so used to reading the Bible as a religious document, and so sure of what is proper within the field of religion and what is not, that we miss a great deal of what the Bible has to say against sanctimonious religiosity. But these fisherfolk do not react in the same way. They realize that what is going on is a big party. One of them observes "isn't it interesting that Jesus gets himself involved for a party? His hour will come sooner because he gave wine at a party. It wasn't for anything more serious." But the most surprising comment is made by a participant who does not speak too often: "If all the water they had for purifying themselves turned into wine on them, now how were they going to perform their ceremonies? I'm sure some of them must have asked him: 'Master, and now how do I purify myself?' And he must have answered them: 'The orders are to have a drink'."[35]

To our minds, trained to believe about Jesus only that which is proper, this seems sacrilegious. But, does it not come closer than most of our interpretations to the spirit of the Master's teachings and to his repeated disapproval of the religious folk of his time?

The same sort of insight comes from feminist interpretations. Joanna Dewey, after asserting that we must "read the Bible afresh,"[36] proceeds to a study of the beginning of the book of Exodus from which she draws unexpected, but well substantiated conclusions:

> Certainly in both the story about the midwives and the story of the women's rescue of the baby, the women are acting independently and not as adjuncts of men.
> In both stories the actions of the women are actions of disobedience to the authority of Pharaoh. . . . And in both stories the disobedience results in deliverance: The disobedience of the midwives saves the Hebrew people; the disobedience of the mother, sister, and Pharaoh's daughter saves Moses. . . .
> And if God was later acting through Moses to deliver the people, then God first of all acted through these women to deliver the people. Women as well as men are God's agents of salvation and, in the story of the exodus, God's first agents.[37]

When one reads the biblical account, one is driven to conclude that she is right. And yet, how many of us have heard sermons stating this fact? By bringing their own experience to bear on the reading of the texts, Dewey and other women are offering the entire church new insights into the biblical message.

Some of these insights have to do with the impact of Jesus' teaching on the commonly accepted views regarding women. Those women who have become conscious of the manner in which they are usually stereotyped object to the prevalent view that a woman is to be defined above all else in her roles as mother and wife. They do not object to those options, nor do they seek to demean their value, just as no male would object to the options and the value of being a husband and a father. What they reject is the notion that, while such roles are not all that a man is expected to be, women are often seen only as real, potential, or frustrated wives and mothers. This obviously serves to keep women at home in their subservient roles, and to prevent them from competing with men in other fields of endeavor. As in other such cases, the traditional interpretation of the Bible leads one to believe that the women who object to such stereotyping will find no support in Scripture. But exactly the opposite is shown by women such as Rachel Conrad Wahlberg, who focuses her attention on two well-known passages.

The first of these is Luke 11:27-28: "While he was saying this, a woman in the crowd raised her voice and said to him, 'Blessed is the womb that bore you, and the breasts that nursed you!' But he said, 'Blessed rather are those who hear the word of God and obey it!'"(NRSV).

Most traditional interpretation centers on the fact that Jesus corrected the woman. Others use this text as an argument against the excessive veneration of Mary. But Rachel Conrad Wahlberg points out that here Jesus is rejecting the stereotype of a woman as first of all a reproductive being:

> Subsequent centuries have been so accepting of the stereotyped woman that they have not noticed what Jesus said. Religious interpreters have not known what to do with this radical rejection by Jesus of the uterus image. Does he mean to put down the idea of woman as child-bearer? Is he demeaning her function as a fetus-carrier and a baby-suckler?
>
> Remember that only if a woman had children, and preferably boys, was she honored. If she were "barren" she was regarded as one to be pitied. Actually her status in that society was based on the uterus image. Her worth *was* in her procreativeness.
>
> It is mind-blowing to realize that Jesus was actually rejecting this commonly accepted justification for the existence of woman. If not a child-bearer, what was woman? Jesus is saying: *She is one who can hear the will of God and do it.*[38]

The same author deals with the woman-as-wife stereotype when discussing Mark 12:18-25 and its parallel texts in Matthew and Luke. That is the familiar story of the Sadducees who posed to Jesus the question of the man who died and left a wife, but no children. She was then married in succession to six brothers of her late husband, all of whom died leaving no issue. The question that the Sadducees posed was, whose wife will she be in the resurrection? And Jesus' answer is well known: "When they rise from the dead, they neither marry nor are given in marriage, but are like angels in heaven."

This text is usually interpreted in the sense that in heaven there will be no sexuality. Some males have even understood it to mean that in heaven women will be unnecessary! But when a woman reads this text, she sees much more in it. The question posed by the Sadducees was based on the view of a woman as primarily a wife and someone's possession. It is significant that the question does not start by referring to "a woman who was widowed," but to "seven brothers." The important question is not what will happen to the woman herself. The question is rather that she *belongs* to seven different brothers in this life, and that therefore in the next it will be difficult to decide to which of the seven brothers she belongs. For all intents and purposes, the story could have been about seven brothers who successively inherited a cow from each other. A woman who knows that society stereotypes a woman as "someone's wife" will see in this text much more than will a man.

A woman hears about a durable woman who outlived seven husbands.

A woman hears that this person was someone's property—*seven someones.*

A woman hears that this someone was passed from brother to brother perhaps without her approval, because it was the Deuteronomic law and custom.

A woman understands that not having children would have placed an added stigma on the woman.

A woman hears that Jesus, although he says nothing about levirate marriage, disclaims the dependency of the marriage bond in the resurrection.

A woman hears Jesus declaring that she is not someone's property, that she has equal status in the resurrection, that she has a position not relative to anyone else. She is a spiritual being. At least in heaven she will not achieve her identity through someone else.[39]

From the Third World come other insights. Some of these are profound in their simplicity. Take for instance the words of Catholic Bishop Christopher Mwoleka of Tanzania:

I think we have problems understanding the Holy Trinity because we approach the mystery from the wrong side. The intellectual side is not the best side to start with. We try to get hold of the wrong end of the stick, and it never works. The right approach to the mystery is to *imitate* the Trinity. We keep making the mistake Philip made by asking: "Rabbi, show us the Father!" Christ was dismayed by the question and rebuked Philip: "Philip, have I been with you so long and yet you don't know me? He who has seen me has seen the Father. How can you say: show us the Father? Do you not believe that I am in the Father and the Father in me?" Then Christ continued to say: "He who believes in me will also do the works that I do, and greater works than these will he do."

On believing in this mystery, the first thing we should have done was to imitate God, then we would ask no more questions, for we would understand. God does not reveal Himself to us for the sake of speculation. He is not giving us a riddle to solve. He is offering us life. He is telling us: "This is what it means to live, now begin to live as I do." What is the one and only reason why God revealed this mystery to us if it is not to stress that life is not life at all unless it is shared?

If we would once begin to share life in all its aspects, we would soon understand what the Trinity is all about and rejoice. . . .

Why did God upon creating human beings not put us straight into heaven, but instead put us here on earth? The reason why we should first have to wait here for a number of years before going to heaven would seem to be that we should practice and acquire some competence in the art of sharing life. Without this practice we are apt to mess up things in heaven. . . . All I want to say is this: it is by sharing the earthly goods that we come to have an idea of what it will be like to share the life of God.

As long as we do not know how to share earthly goods, as God would have us do, it is an illusion to imagine that we know what it is to share the life of the Trinity which is our destiny. . . .

The question is: Have we imitated the Holy Trinity in sharing earthly goods? . . . Could I truthfully say: "All mine are thine, and thine are mine," to each and all? This is what we are supposed to imitate (John 17:10). Then in what sense can we be said to be practicing to live the life of God? How can we dare to profess the religion of the Trinity?[40]

As we read these words, do we not sense a kinship between the Tanzanian bishop and some of the writers that we quoted in the previous section, such as Ambrose and Basil the Great? Is it a mere coincidence that those theologians of old, who so stressed the need for a different social order, were also among the champions of Trinitarian theology? Or could it be that we have been misled in our reading of the history of theology, and that the doctrine of the Trinity, far from being the purely speculative matter that we have been led to believe, was part and parcel of those preachers' radical theology? This is an intriguing question which would bear investigation. But in any case, there is no doubt that Bishop Mwoleka has given us an insight into the significance of Trinitarian theology that we are not likely to derive from many Western theologians.

Some Korean theologians have developed "minjung" theology, or theology from the perspective of the suffering community.[41] Central to this theology is *han*, a complex concept pointing to the experience of unjust suffering, of being the victim of sin or evil. Han can be produced in individuals, but it is also the experience of whole groups of people, often because of their sex, nationality, or race. It is also the burden of the poor and despised.

Andrew Sung Park, a Korean-American theologian, has written an illuminating study of the Christian understanding of sin and the concept of han, pointing out the limitations of most Christian perspectives on sin and salvation that deal only with the sinner rather than also with the victims of sin. He uses the perspective of han to expand our understanding of both sin and redemption. In so doing, he sheds new light on several biblical passages. For instance, he writes:

> The parable of the prodigal son shows the bilateral character of salvation. From the son's view, salvation is "justification by faith" through the grace of the father. From the father's view, salvation is the resolution of han. This story shows us that salvation lies in the healing of the relationship between the father and the son. We have ignored the dimension of salvation needed for the father, the victim of sin.[42]

Park finds the concept of han useful not only in biblical interpretation, but also in the reappropriation of tradition. He sees Anselm's view of atonement as taking seriously the pain or han of God caused by human sin. God is the victim of our sin, and is wounded by it. The cross is God's active means of bringing about reconciliation so that both the sin of humanity and the han of God can be overcome.[43]

For too long the theological and ecclesiastical establishment of the North

Atlantic has been doing theology as if the rest of the world did not exist or had only the secondary sort of existence of the Lone Ranger's Tonto. Tonto has finally decided to speak up. And he is making much more sense that the Lone Ranger ever did! The Lone Ranger, with his mask, his white horse, and his flashy gear, thought that he knew all about doing justice. But Tonto is telling him that one can only know injustice when one suffers it. The only way one can have real access to the resources mentioned in this chapter, and to others like them, is to join the Tontos of our day in the struggle against injustice, and to join them in such a way as to be deprived of white horses and flashy gear. Do-gooder preaching is out. Cries of "hi-ho, Silver" will no longer do. The word of the gospel today, as in the times of Jesus, as ever, comes to us most clearly in the painful groans of the oppressed. We must listen to those groans. We must join the struggle to the point where we too must groan. Or we may choose the other alternative, which is not to hear the gospel at all.

IV

Some Pointers
on Biblical Interpretation

In the foregoing chapters, while discussing various issues, we have given a number of examples of liberating readings of biblical texts. This is crucial, for Scripture and its interpretation remain the pivotal factor in preaching a liberating message. Many such examples come from neglected interpreters in earlier Christian traditions. Others come from our own contemporaries, as they read the Bible from the perspectives of their own struggles. It is important for preachers to be aware of these various interpretations. They serve as clues to the possible opening up of a passage in different, more liberating ways. They should also provide encouragement for preachers and other interpreters to go and do likewise, that is, to feel free to follow the insights of their own perspectives into the meaning of biblical passages.

This last point is important. Our purpose is not to have all preachers, in whatever circumstances, agree with and follow our interpretation of particular passages. On the contrary, the very fact that different perspectives bring out different elements in the text means that there are many different, yet accurate interpretations of any one text. At the same time, however, this does not mean that no interpretation is wrong—one must be careful not to try to force the text to carry a load it will not bear. Thus, our purpose here is to encourage each preacher, in her or his own concrete setting, to read and proclaim Scripture in a way that is liberating and true to the text itself.

In order to encourage preachers to do so, we offer the "pointers" that appear in this chapter. Note, however, that they are only "pointers." We do not claim the higher status of "methods," and even less do we pretend to provide a systematic approach to biblical hermeneutics. Our goal is much more humble. We intend the pointers as hints or clues that preachers may follow as they seek to break texts open for liberation. Since we do not seek to provide a systematic approach to hermeneutics, the pointers may overlap with each other, so that more than one may be helpful in the interpretation of a particular text, and some may not apply at all to some texts.

Read the Political Situation

Marshall McLuhan was right. In some sense, "the medium is the message."[1] In the case of preaching, the medium includes the social, political, and economic identity of the preacher. The message is also shaped in part by the social, political, and economic identity of the congregation. We must begin by raising the political question, not only about characters in the biblical text—as will be shown in the next section—but also about the characters in the event of preaching itself—the preacher and the congregation.

Most of us assume that if we wish to know what a word means, a look in the dictionary will answer our question. Obviously, this is true as far a definitions are concerned. But as to what is communicated by that word, we need to look at more than the dictionary. Words do not stand alone. They are spoken by one person to another. The social relationship, the dynamic of power that exists between speaker and hearer in the wider society, makes an enormous difference as to what is communicated. It is not enough to know the words. For instance, listen to the words: "Be satisfied with what you have. Do not be greedy." We can easily know what they mean in the abstract. Yet if we imagine them being spoken in a middle-class white church by a guest preacher who is the pastor of a poor African American church, they would mean one thing; and they would means something quite different if spoken by the pastor of an affluent white church while preaching to a poor African American congregation. In one case there is a clear rebuke to those who already have more than others. In the other, the one who has more is rebuking the aspirations for equality of those who have less.

The problem grows even greater when the powerful have many more opportunities to address the powerless, than the powerless to address the powerful. Yet that is clearly the case, for the powerful control more media, publish more books, give more lectures, chair more committees, and financially support more causes than do the powerless. And on the rare occasions when the powerless are invited to address the powerful, this is often treated by the powerful as a charitable or a liberal action on their part. Little of significance can be communicated under those circumstances.

Those who are usually considered powerless by society are well aware of such dynamics in communication. The woman who preaches does not have to be told that her identity as female will be perceived by the congregation and will be a factor in interpreting what she says. The minority person will be equally conscious of the effect of ethnic identity on the hearing of words. For both the woman and the minority person this sense of the significance of identity will be present whether they are speaking to a group composed of those who are like themselves, or to a group of the powerful. Always it matters and is a factor. Yet many white male preachers remain oblivious to such considerations, unless they are thrown into the situation of preaching to a minority church. The rest of the time, to be white and male seems to them to have no particular effect on the words spoken and heard. Yet that is not the case. In the act of preaching, the social and political situation of speaker and hearer are part of the context that gives meaning to the words that are spoken.

This is one of the reasons why, when preaching to groups other than their own, both women and minority preachers are generally more biblical in their preaching than are many other people. They know quite well that when they preach, they do not have the benefit of status conferred upon them by society at large. In fact, the stereotypes are such that they realistically expect that they will be thought quite ignorant and incapable of conveying a significant message. Under such circumstances, aside from any theological opinion that would lead them to be more radically biblical in their preaching, the explication and application of a specific biblical text becomes their chief source of authority, in a way and to a degree that is not necessary for the white male preacher. The white male preacher has general credibility unless he shows himself to be incompetent. Therefore, he may be tempted to rely on public presence, jokes, irrelevant illustrations, voice characteristic, and so forth, and not on the biblical text itself. Those to whom society gives no such initial credibility find that they cannot rely on such extraneous matters, particularly when preaching to a congregation composed mostly of those whom society considers powerful and informed. Their only authority will be in the biblical text, which must come through clearly and unambiguously in their preaching. Only then can they expect a hearing. White males who decide to preach on the radical demands of Scripture may soon find themselves in a similar situation. This is one of the reasons why liberation theology can lead to a biblical renewal in the task and art of preaching. In fact, as the church as a whole becomes more marginal in our society, all preachers will be driven to rely more clearly on the biblical text. The converse is also true: it is quite likely that the more obedient to Scripture a church seeks to be, the more the powerful will seek to marginalize it.

On the other hand, the matter is more complicated: the powerful and the powerless are not neatly separated into distinct congregations. Though our churches are frequently composed of only one race and ethnic group, and though they frequently reflect a limited spectrum in terms of economic status, they are all composed of both men and women, and the factor of power and powerlessness between the sexes is present in all of them. Many of the women are currently struggling with their own roles, in a strong or hesitant fashion. If the preacher is male and much of the congregation is female, the words of the speaker will probably convey something very different to many of the women than what they convey to most of the men who hear the same sermon. A pastor who is aware of such dynamics can make the communication far clearer and avoid being misunderstood, by either the powerful or the powerless in the congregation.

For instance, a male preacher may preach on Mark 8:34 and stress the need to be selfless, to be constantly in the service of others rather than concerned for ourselves. Of course there is truth to this message. It is a necessary and central element of the gospel. These words will probably be heard by many men as the pastor intends. However, if a woman in the congregation is considering returning to school and is struggling with the issue of how this will affect the family, she will probably hear these words as a rebuke to her new sense of possibility for herself. Her plans are selfish and therefore unchristian. She must continue to serve her family in the old way and not think about herself. On the other hand the presence of a woman in the pulpit, no matter what she says, may be a call and an inspiration for the woman in the pew to explore her own capabilities.

Do we wish to equate Christian self-denial with the traditional role of the powerless? Are we really wishing to claim that subservience should continue and that any thought of self-determination is sinful? Surely that is not the case. Nor were the male pastor's words intended to reinforce the traditional roles and curb change. In fact, he may have thought his words would have the opposite effect and serve to rebuke the rest of the family for loading the work on the wife and mother. One of the most frequent breakdowns in communication comes when the powerful are rebuked from the pulpit by a pastor who is one of their number. Truly prophetic preaching needs to do this rebuking on occasion. But the same words, if there is no clear awareness of the political dimensions, can have the effect of saying to the powerless who also hear the message that it is sinful to try to alter the status quo. By implication, the powerless hear that, as Christians, they must stay in their place. A few direct comments could avoid such misunderstanding. The preacher can indicate for what human condition the message is appropriate. Possible mistaken understandings can be explicitly rejected. Only if the preacher is aware of these political dynamics within the congregation can the danger be avoided. The use of clear contemporary examples that do not perpetuate stereotypes is another way of lessening such misunderstandings.

What is said here about sermons also applies to prayers. Particularly in prayers of confession, all the political factors, the different meanings the same words can have when heard by the powerless rather than by the powerful for whom they were intended, come into play. For instance, thinking more highly of ourselves than we ought to think is more typically a sin of the powerful. The powerless usually have problems with a low self-image, and a sense that they probably cannot succeed at much of significance. The same prayer that can genuinely convict a powerful person can have the negative and theologically inaccurate result of increasing the low self-esteem of the powerless. It is not that pride should never be confessed. Rather it should be made clear what is not meant by the words. The powerless have their own sins, and these do not often make their way into our prayers of confession: false humility, refusal to take on God-given responsibility, for instance. Rarely do these appear in prayers of confession written by the powerful, since these are not the sins which generally tempt them. A humble prayer of thanksgiving that remembers gratefully "all that God has given us" may look different to the dispossessed who are not the least bit sure God did give it to those who have it. In their eyes, we and our society as a whole may well have taken much of what God had actually intended for them. Think, for instance, of the typical prayers in a Thanksgiving Day service in a white church, and consider whether you would offer the same prayer if there were a group of Native Americans present.

The matter is further complicated by the fact that people cannot be identified simply as powerful or powerless. We have mentioned it before, and yet it must constantly be kept in mind. The white woman struggling for new possibilities still must remember that she is also an oppressor when it comes to the Third World or ethnic minorities within her own society. The same awareness of being cast in the role of oppressor by the Third World must be there for the minority person in our country. Even the white, male, middle-class American is in a way caught and oppressed. Liberation theology will function helpfully in a congregation only if the myriad of political dynamics present there are made clear and addressed by the gospel. A blanket pronouncement lacks the historical particularity that is one of the hallmarks of such theology. A preacher must be specific, or the use of such theology is at best irrelevant and at worst oppressive.

Since women are the clearest example of the traditionally powerless who are present in most of our congregations, the issue of gender-specific language cannot be avoided. Gender problems arise in most languages, but English has its own peculiarities. There are many books and articles that offer suggestions for correcting the constant use of "man," "mankind," etc., as though these words automatically included women. There has also been significant work done on the alternatives to the constant use of masculine imagery and pronouns for God. These books and articles also give the rationale for such changes. It is not necessary here to dwell on the specifics of the language changes that are needed. Suffice it to say that the male pastor who does use inclusive language, who does acknowledge the validity of the issue, has taken a political stand that will be noticed and supported by those in the congregation who are struggling with the need for new roles for women. Conversely, any male pastor who does not make changes in his language is also communicating a political message of support for the traditional oppressive arrangement, whether he is conscious of this or not. The congregation will be quite aware of either message. It is because of this awareness that so much emotion is expended by those who do and do not want change. The preacher has no choice but to take a stand. The content of what is said will be interpreted partly by the context provided by the choice of language. That is to say, a male pastor who thinks he is quite liberating in his preaching but whose language remains unreconstructed will find that a certain skepticism greets his statements, whereas a pastor who does use careful language will be given the benefit of the doubt by those women who feel oppressed, even when some of his statements could otherwise be misinterpreted. Changing language is not enough for liberating preaching, but exclusive language can blunt such preaching disastrously, at least as far as women are concerned, and they are the largest powerless group present in most congregations.

All that has been said refers to the male preacher. The female minister is not in quite the same situation. Obviously it is to be hoped and expected that she will use inclusive language. This will generally be the case. But if she does not, the fact of who she is—a woman in the pulpit—speaks so loudly against the traditional stereotypes of what women should be that her impact is still very different from that of a man who uses masculine language.

Include the Wider Context

Women are present in all congregations, but some of the most significant powerless groups are not present in our congregations on Sunday morning. Their absence is explained by several obvious reasons. First of all, one group is Third World people who simply live in another part of the globe. Their absence is hardly surprising. A second group may well be those of a different ethnic group or class who live in the neighborhood but are members of other congregations. This division is characteristic of our society, and should be overcome. But trying to woo members of one congregation into another is hardly the way to do it. How churches in the community can have a positive relationship with one another across racial and economic lines is the issue, rather than how these church members can change their local church membership.

There are situations where a white, middle-class congregation and pastor see the need for evangelism and mission in their own area among unchurched people who would be classified by the society as marginal and powerless. With such a goal, a pastor may discover that preaching geared to

71

the powerful, even the repentant powerful, may be alienating and oppressive to any member of the powerless group who happens to attend the service. Here again, as in the case of the women in the congregation, the preacher must be well aware of the political dynamics that affect how what is said will actually be heard by the various members of the congregation, given their concrete situations. The powerless may be absent precisely because they know that they are not taken seriously when they are present. One goes to church to hear the gospel preached to one's own condition, not to overhear it preached to others.

The actual preaching heard by the rare member of a powerless group who attends the service is not the major way in which preaching relates to the absent powerless. The mission of the church in the world is not carried out primarily by the preacher from the pulpit. Yet the mission of the church is not totally divorced from that preaching either. One of the major tasks that must be done in congregations composed of groups classified as powerful is to have such congregations develop an awareness of how they are viewed by the powerless. The mission of the church cannot be carried out authentically until there is such an understanding. This is most particularly true at present among the churches that have traditionally sent missionaries and the younger churches in the Third World. It is equally true in our own country among white churches and those of ethnic minorities. A sensitive preacher can help a congregation enormously in this respect.

This means that part of the task of preaching, as well as part of the preparation for it, is to ask the question, How would this biblical text be heard and applied authentically by someone in a radically different political and social setting? It is not only the preacher who needs to be aware of such interpretations in order to develop a more adequate theology; the congregation needs to develop the same skill in order to discover more adequately its mission in the world and how that mission can be carried out. The congregation is not helped unless the preacher uses some very clear examples.

For instance, think about the parable of the workers in the vineyard, all of whom receive the same wage, though they have labored very different amounts of time (Matt. 20:1-16). Most people in most congregations in the United States find this a text to avoid. It runs against our grain and seems quite unfair. We can probably understand that in regard to God all of us are those who were hired late, who have received from God far more than we deserve. But we prefer the way the parable of the Prodigal Son makes the same point. Yet when we imagine a group of Chicano migrant workers, waiting at the appointed place to be hired, perhaps, for the day, the parable begins to look quite different. For those who frequently find no work, for those who never know in the morning if there will be any wages at the end of the day, the parable would communicate the great justice, not the unfairness of God. The congregation needs to see this, and by so doing, the absent powerless will be brought into their midst.

Furthermore, once this aspect of the text is seen, then it becomes easier to see the relation of this particular parable to its setting in Matthew. Is it accidental that it follows immediately on a section (Matt. 19:16-30) that begins with the rich young ruler and ends with disciples concerned about whether it was worthwhile to give up all they had in order to follow Jesus? Between these two stand the harsh words about how hard it is for the rich to enter the Kingdom. Both the section in Matthew 19 and the parable in 20 end with the cryptic words about the first being last, and the last first.

The presence in the sermon and therefore in the minds of the congregation of those migrant workers can begin to make clear where many of the rest of us fit into the text. The place of those whom the landlord unexpectedly rewards is taken by these others, and we are left in the more difficult situation of being the ones rebuked because we begrudge the generosity of the landlord. How do we respond to the rebuke? Do we feel that we deserve it? What does this say about how we ought to live out our faith in the world? Our dislike of the parable can then be understood and dealt with. It is a text that comes to life much more readily when the absent powerless are brought into the presence of the congregation.

It would be far easier for most of us if the church were limited to our own nation. Then we could avoid the situation of having the same Bible read and meditated upon by those who see us as their enemies or oppressors because of the economic and political relationships of our nation and its economy to those of the poorer countries of the world. It would be easier if those who are hungry did not include Christians who feel that we, their fellow Christians, are in some ways the cause of their hunger. But because these unpleasant facts are a reality, we are faced with the situation that many Christians in other parts of the world, as they read their Bibles and identify readily with the oppressed and the downtrodden, place us in the role of the enemies in the text. We cannot ignore their interpretation, but rather must seek to determine the justice of their reaction and ways to overcome both the reality and the hostility that ensues. We are indeed called to be part of the same Body of Christ, united by one faith, one baptism, and one Lord. The political situation in which we find ourselves destroys that unity much more than many of the differences in doctrine that have divided the church in the past. Our mission as the church is hindered in the world because of these political factors. Were we ever as the church able to establish strong communication across these political lines, were we able to come to agreement as to what is actually the truth about our relationship to one another in the present world, the church could be a dynamic force for peace in the whole world and its message would be more convincing. But in reality, we Christians are as divided by the political dynamics as are any other people. If in a local congregation our brothers and sisters in the faith who now stand in a hostile relationship to us were actually made present, if we could begin to see the gospel from their point of view, then actually creating links with them would be far more of a possibility. The preacher has more opportunity to make this a reality than does almost anyone else in the church.

There seems to be a common model of preaching today that concerns itself only with the needs of those who are physically present in the congregation. This is seen as primarily pastoral. Obviously, the spiritual and material needs of the visible congregation need to be taken into consideration by the preacher. However, where the needs of those present are the main focus of preaching, the needs of those who are absent are missing, and the whole concept of the mission of the church is lost.

The relation of power and missions is complex. Yet it is true to say that in the past five or six hundred years, the branches of the Christian church that have developed missionary consciousness have been precisely in those countries that were beginning to make their power felt in the rest of the world: Spain and Portugal in the sixteenth century, Great Britain and the United States in the nineteenth and twentieth centuries. Part of the reason is that world-consciousness developed within the church in nations where the society was experiencing its own expansion into other parts of the globe. There also was money for such missionary ventures as the society expanded economically and politically.

This means, however, that as the issues of power and powerlessness become acute between First and Third World nations today, relationships are complicated between the churches that once sent missionaries and those that were founded by those missionaries in the past. In our own churches in the United States, the issue of what the overseas mission of the church ought to be and how it should be carried out has been both critical and divisive in the past few years. Very often there seems to be a breakdown in communication between boards of mission at the national level and local congregations. National boards are generally aware of the radically changed circumstances in a world where many of the traditionally powerless people are demanding drastic alterations in the balance between nations and between churches. Often such new understandings at the national level are not communicated or else are rejected by local congregations that still see the world in an earlier framework, where our country sent missionaries, determined what they would do, and had great success. They see no reason to change now. In fact, whatever conditions cause such change must be demonic! Now these younger churches demand much more autonomy, and even suggest that it would be helpful if our churches received missionaries from the powerless church who clearly have a word to speak as to the meaning of the gospel in our day. Such words are very difficult for many Christians in this country.

The pastor whose preaching begins to accustom a congregation to hearing such words has made great strides in enabling the mission of the church to go forward in the midst of a very new reality in the world. Such preaching could also begin to heal divisions within denominations caused by differing world-views and assumptions. To bring the absent powerless into the sermon wherever they belong in the biblical text can have these effects.

Consider the Politics of the Text

Having taken into account the politics of the preaching act, it is also necessary to look at the political dynamics within the text itself. Obviously, "political" is not understood here in the common usage of whether to vote for one candidate or for another, although it does have to do with that. By "political" we mean rather the interplay of power, the question of who is expected to have authority over whom, or of who is an "insider" and who is not. "Political" means above all, in this context, the manner in which God intervenes in such relations, and how God responds to the power or powerlessness of various individuals or groups of people. To ask this question at the outset may serve to counteract the opposite, more common interpretation, which acts as if such matters were of no consequence, and thus serves to entrench the powerful in their positions of privilege.

In some cases the political dimension is rather evident. Such is, for instance, the case of the prophet Amos in his relationship to Jeroboam, king of Israel, and to Amaziah, the priest of Bethel, which culminates in Amos 7:12-15:

> And Amaziah said to Amos, "O seer, go, flee away to the land of Judah, earn your bread there, and prophesy there; but never again prophesy at Bethel, for it is the king's sanctuary, and it is a temple of the kingdom."
> Then Amos answered Amaziah, "I am no prophet, nor a prophet's son; but I am a herdsman, and a dresser of sycamore trees, and the Lord took me from following the flock, and the Lord said to me, 'Go, prophesy to my people Israel.' " (NRSV)

Preachers often note, quite correctly, that Amaziah was the mouthpiece of official religion, which as usual was being used to uphold the status quo, and that he was afraid of the implications of what Amos was saying. Often missed is that Amaziah attempted to use the power and prestige of Jeroboam to silence the disturbing prophet. Thus, it is not simply a matter of official religion supporting the structures of oppression, but also of those structures supporting that form of religion which they find most useful.

There is, however, another dimension that is often hardly noticed. When Amos says that he is not a prophet nor a prophet's son, but a herdsman and a dresser of sycamore trees, he is not simply saying that God called him to preach out of another occupation. This text is often used to highlight the experience of a middle-aged and successful businessman who leaves his company in order to become a minister. That may be a legitimate use; but it is important to note that Amos is not simply telling Amaziah that he was doing something else when God called him. He is rather responding to the priest's ominous words from the perspective of a powerless one whom God has empowered. Amaziah tells him that he is interfering with what is going on at Bethel, and that he must remember that this place is "the king's sanctuary, and it is a temple of the kingdom." He also recommends—much like a gangster "recommends" caution to someone whose testimony could prove troublesome—that the prophet return to his native Judah, and that he prophesy there—which after all, is his home turf. He further implies that the prophet has come to Bethel seeking personal gain, and he therefore suggests that Amos go and earn his bread in Judah. In short, Amaziah's words are both a threat and a putdown. But Amos responds as someone speaking from the perspective of the powerless who have been empowered by God. He must reject the priest's suggestion, not because Bethel is a more productive place for prophets—after all, he is not really a prophet—nor because he himself has power or authority—he is a herdsman and a dresser of sycamore trees—but because he has been commanded and empowered from on high. He says, in effect, "You are a priest, and I do not even belong to the class of professional prophets. I am nothing but a herdsman and an agricultural laborer. And out of that situation, in backward Judah, the Lord took me and sent me to prophesy to mighty, rich, and proud Israel." When all these political implications are seen, the text has a bite that it did not have when we simply applied it to the successful businessman turned preacher.

In other cases the political dimension may not be as evident; but it is still there. Take for instance the story of Rahab, as told in the book of Joshua. The fact that she was a harlot is the one detail that all remember, either because it rubs against our moral standards or because it appeals to our prurient interests. Others point out that through faith her entire family was saved, and establish a parallel with the jailer at Philippi. But few take note of the political dimensions involved in the story. In a sense, what we have here is simply a case of treason. Rahab betrays the people of Jericho, her own city. It may well be at this point that being a harlot is significant. The word used for her is not the one which refers to the more respected religious prostitutes. As a harlot, although perhaps not as condemned as modern prostitutes, she certainly was not one of the powerful in Jericho. And when the opportunity came, she sided with the God who empowered the nomadic and, from the point of view of Jericho, semibarbaric Israelites. It is significant that John Calvin, who had to leave his beloved country because of his faith, saw the political implications of Rahab's action and saw also that faith may lead one to break the civil law:

> When, therefore, Rahab knew that the object intended was the over-
> throw of the city in which she had been born and brought up, it seems a
> detestable act of inhumanity to give her aid and counsel to the spies. . . .
> Therefore, although she had been bound to her countrymen up to that
> very day, yet when she was adopted into the body of the Church, her new
> condition was a kind of manumission from the common law by which
> citizens are bound toward each other.[2]

In Acts 2:1-42 we have the story of Pentecost. It is a well-known story, and yet one which gains new significance when we approach it asking the political question. When we do this, there are at least three elements that come to the foreground.

The first has to do with the commonplace juxtaposition between this text and the story of the tower of Babel in Genesis 11:1-9. In this context, it is often said that Pentecost undoes the confusion of Babel; that human pride in Babel causes confusion, and that divine action in Pentecost brings unity. That may be true up to a point; but there is much more that must be said. Note, for instance, that in the story of Pentecost the disciples are together, apparently in quite an orderly fashion, at the beginning of the story, and that towards the end, before Peter's speech, there is confusion (the NRSV translates: "amazed and perplexed") among those who witness the event. Note also that, even apart from the miracle, those who witness it apparently have some sort of common language, for they clearly are able to communicate with each other (Acts 2:12). Therefore, what Pentecost brings about is not simply unity where there was not, but rather a different sort of unity where empire and conquest had already produced their own unity. Pentecost even confuses the unity which already exists. From the perspective of the powerful, who benefit from the unity and order of society, Pentecost is interpreted as simply reinforcing that order and unity. From the opposite perspective, Pentecost destroys that unity and brings about a different sort.

Second, note that the hearers from various countries are not all made to understand the language of the disciples. The outsiders, those from Parthia, Media, Elam, etc., are not made to conform to the insiders. On the contrary, "each one heard them speaking in the native language of each" (Acts 2:6). When we read this passage from the political context at the close of the twentieth century in the United States, where there is increasing debate as to the place of languages other than English in American society, and the need for cultural unity and uniformity, what stands out is that the Spirit did not require that all come to understand the language of the original community, but on the contrary, made certain that all heard in their own languages. In other words, that if in the early church there was any hint of an "Aramaic-only" movement, at Pentecost the Spirit responded with a resounding "No!"

Third, Peter's interpretation of the event itself, based on the passage from

Joel, makes it clear that the Spirit is no respecter of privilege. The Spirit is poured "upon all flesh," and this includes sons as well as daughters, young as well as old, and male and female slaves.

Another passage which comes to mind as an example of the significance of political considerations is Acts 6:1-6. The story told there has to do with a conflict that arose in the early church, for apparently the widows of the "Hellenists" were not receiving the same treatment as the widows of the "Hebrews." In fact, they are all Jewish. The difference is that some are more connected with the Diaspora, and others with Palestine. While one group is probably more at home in Aramaic, the other prefers Greek. But that is not all. This was a time of growing nationalism among Jews—a nationalism that would lead to open rebellion, and eventually to the destruction of the Temple. In that situation, Hellenistic Jews were regarded askance by the more traditional Aramaic-speaking Jews from Palestine. After all, there was abundant biblical evidence that when Israel was unfaithful, God chastised the nation by bringing in foreign powers to rule over it. Therefore, in order to regain independence, Israel and all the people must be absolutely faithful. From the perspective of the "Hebrews," the "Hellenists" were not quite as strict as they should be in their religious observance. As a result, the Hellenists were seen, not only as outsiders, but also as less religious, and probably partly responsible for the woes of the nation.

Now that division, which is present in the nation at large, has found its way into the church, and there are complaints (NRSV) or murmuring (KJV), that the widows of the Hellenists are not receiving their fair share of that which is being distributed among the needy. If it were today, we would begin by speaking of the "problem" of the Hellenist widows. But the fact of the matter is that the "problem" was not caused by the Hellenistic widows, but by the Spirit of God, who has the nasty habit of bringing outsiders in, as was shown on that day of Pentecost. Or, supposing that our church is somewhat enlightened, we would probably attempt to deal with the "problem" by appointing a token Hellenist to the Finance Committee. Or, if we are even more enlightened, we would set a minimum quota of Hellenists in the Committee. Or, if we really are avant-garde, we would set aside a portion of our benevolence funds, and make it available to the Hellenists, to disburse as they see fit. But what that early church does is none of the above. It names a committee to distribute the funds, and *all* its members have Greek names! As a matter of fact, one is not even Jewish by birth, for we are told that he was "a proselyte of Antioch." This is so startling, that commentators have sought to improve on what the text says by claiming that the "seven" were a parallel institution to the "twelve," so that the seven became the leaders and managers for the Hellenists, while the twelve retained a parallel position among the "Hebrews."[3] The text, however, gives no hint of that, and therefore one suspects that such commentators have hidden and subconscious agendas. In any case, it is apparent that the text, when read in this fashion, has important implications for the manner in which churches today deal with ethnic and cultural minorities in their own midst—an issue that is becoming increasingly important for churches in the Unites States, but which has implications for churches throughout the world.

If one looks at the politics of that text from a different perspective, other issues arise. The twelve ask the church to name seven *men*, and that is precisely what the church does. But the twelve also declare that the seven will be responsible for the distribution, while they, the twelve, will reserve for themselves the ministry of preaching. Yet, hardly has their election taken place, when Acts tells us that Stephen, one of the seven, is preaching. Indeed, Stephen's sermon is the longest in the entire book of Acts. And he is not supposed to be preaching! Apparently, we learn from the Acts of the Apostles that the freedom of the Spirit cannot be curtailed, and that even though the twelve wished to reserve for themselves the ministry of the Word, the Spirit had other ideas. By reading the text in this fashion, one can reasonably argue that the same Spirit who went beyond the designs of the twelve, and turned Stephen (and then Philip) into a preacher, has more recently broken the other design, that only *men* be appointed.

We have already referred to the story of Simon Magus in Acts 8. It is noteworthy that, although the text itself says that Simon "amazed the people of Samaria," and that all, "from the least to the greatest," said of him that "this man is that power of God which is called great," the standard interpretation of the entire incident leaves aside all question of power and powerlessness and prefers to speak of Simon as a hypocrite, when the text says nothing about that. In fact, what the text does say is that Simon believed and was baptized, and that he who used to amaze all was himself amazed. When we ask the political question of this text, it would seem that Simon Magus' problems had to do with power, rather than with disbelief or hypocrisy. And then the intervention of Simon Peter, the relatively ignorant fisherman from Galilee, takes on a new shade of meaning. Simon Magus cannot have "part or share in this," not because he is a hypocrite, but rather because he is a powerful man who wishes to carry that power into his position in the life of the church.

Still in Acts 8, the reader may wish to ask the political question of the other major incident in this chapter, the encounter between Philip and the Ethiopian eunuch. Was the latter an insider, an outsider, or both? What does the text say about his standing in Ethiopia? What do we infer about his standing in Judaism, on the basis of what the Law said about eunuchs? He was reading the prophet Isaiah. What does that prophet have to say about eunuchs and foreigners? In the light of all this, what is the significance of Philip's willingness to baptize this man? What does this say about the nature and mission of the church vis-à-vis the various rules of exclusion in our society?

It would be possible to multiply *ad infinitum* the examples of texts that become clearer when one poses the political question. But the point of this section is more than that. The entire Bible must be read in the light of that question. And this is borne out by the fact that the crucial saving events in both the Old and New Testaments cannot be understood aside from it.

In the Old Testament, the escape from Egypt is an eminently political event. More than that, it is an event in which, in the words of Mary much later, God "has shown strength with his arm, he has scattered the proud in the thoughts of their hearts, he has brought down the mighty from their thrones, and lifted up the lowly" (Luke 1:51-52, NRSV). Apart from that political dimension, the first chapters of the book of Exodus make no sense. And it is a political dimension in which, as Mary saw clearly, God works in a definite direction, against the might of Pharaoh and for the oppressed children of Israel.

Some will respond that such is clearly the case in the Old Testament, which is "materialistic" and lacks the "spiritual" insight of the New. But, aside from the fact that the church very early rejected such contraposition of the two Testaments as heretical, the New Testament is just as political as the Old. It is in part to show this that we have quoted the song of Mary—of Mary, who is usually depicted in quiet, submissive tones that seem to fade into the background! But the entire story of Jesus is profoundly political. God's choice to be born in a stable, to a carpenter's family, rather than in the home of a king or priest, manifests God's politics.

We have already referred to the political naïveté of the magi and its tragic consequences; but there is much in that story that bears more careful political scrutiny. First of all, it is significant that Christian tradition has turned this into a story of "three kings," when in fact in the text there are *two* kings who receive that title: Herod and Jesus. By so doing, traditional interpretation has shifted attention away from the conflict between these two kings, which is at the very heart of the text, and towards three personages who represent imaginary—and therefore non-political—kingdoms. But that is not all. It is bad enough to miss the fact that it was these magi, supposedly wise, who told King Herod of the birth of King Jesus. We also miss the fact that it was the theologians who told him where the birth was to take place (Matt. 2:4-6). The magi tell him when; the theologians, where. Star-gazing, unbiblical religion lends itself to Herod's designs; and so does the biblical scholarship and "sound theology" of the priests and scribes.

Such political dimensions appear throughout the Gospels. Luke states that Jesus was born in Bethlehem because Augustus had decreed a census. Matthew tells us that Jesus was in exile, not only in Egypt, but also through-out his early life, since the reason why he grew up in Nazareth was that he could not return to Judea, then under the authority of Herod's son, Archelaus (Matt. 2:22-23). When Jesus set out on his public ministry, he was constantly at odds with the religious establishment, with which he had a long series of highly political encounters.

One such encounter deserves a separate paragraph, since it has so often been used by those whose political interests lead them to claim that Jesus wanted his followers to accept the existing order of things. It is the incident which concluded with Jesus' words: "Give to the emperor the things that are the emperor's, and to God the things that are God's" (Mark 2:13-17 and parallels). What the supposedly "apolitical" interpreters fail to see is the radically subversive note in Jesus' answer. He did not simply say that it was lawful to pay taxes, and then one could go on to religious things. What he said was that the entire monetary system, because it bore the likeness and the inscription of Caesar, was to be sent back to Caesar, rejected, set aside. He actually refused to condone the practice of those who thought they could cherish Caesar's money, be involved without asking any questions of the entire system, and then debate as to whether they ought to pay taxes or not. In passing one may note that here is another instance in which the study of early Christian literature may be useful. There is a tradition of interpretation, which appears as early as Tertullian,[4] that in this dialogue Jesus was contrasting the image of the emperor on the coin with that of God in humans. There is ample material for reflection along such lines, which would seem to imply that there is a tension between bearing the image of God and paying undue honor to that which bears the image of Caesar.

In the end, these various encounters led to the very political events of the arrest, the trial, and the crucifixion. Caiaphas, Herod, and Pilate are not mere props in a story which would unfold without them. They are main actors. Without them the Gospel narrative would make no sense. And then, beyond the arrest, beyond the trial, beyond the crucifixion, come the most political events in the entire Bible: "God put this power to work in Christ when he raised him from the dead and seated him at his right hand in the heavenly places, far above all rule and authority and power and dominion, and above every name that is named, not only in this age but also in the age to come" (Eph. 1:20-21, NRSV). To call an outlawed and crucified carpenter King of kings and Lord of lords (Rev. 19:16) is a highly political statement.

Reassign the Cast of Characters

Whenever we hear or read a narrative and seek to derive from it some meaning for ourselves, the message conveyed by the story depends in part on where we place ourselves in it. This can be seen clearly in the case of the encounter between King David and the prophet Nathan, after David had Uriah killed in order to cover up his earlier sin, leading to Bethsheba's

81

pregnancy (II Sam. 12:1-15). As is well known, Nathan tells David the story of a rich man who had many sheep, but who killed his poor neighbor's pet lamb in order to feed a visitor. David is enraged and says to Nathan: "As the Lord lives, the man who has done this deserves to die." And it is at this point that Nathan brings the parable home to the king: "You are the man." What has taken place here is that David has been forced to change the place in which he put himself in the story. As long as he though that the prophet had come to him to ask him for justice on behalf of another, he saw himself as the king who was to judge the rich man. But suddenly Nathan tells him that he is the rich man, that it is he who has abused his power, that it is he who, by his own verdict, deserves to die. Thus, the manner in which David assigns the cast of characters in the story has everything to do with the meaning of the story for him. In one case he is the king, the judge, who responds in righteous anger. In the other he is the oppressor who has used his power unjustly and who therefore can only respond, "I have sinned against the Lord."

The same change of perspective takes place for us when we reassign the cast of characters in the parables of Jesus. Many of them are directed against the blindness of the religious leaders of the time, who could not see the inbreaking of God's Reign in the teaching and actions of Jesus. When we read those parables, our normal reaction is to take for granted that, because we are followers of Jesus, we understand what they are all about. Today's Pharisees are those who reject Jesus, who do not attend church, who make a living by peddling pornography, etc. But is this really so? In Jesus' time there were also many who were irreligious or pagan; but the parables were not critical of them. In Jesus' time there were also those who did not keep the religious observances set forth in the Law and who hardly ever went to the Temple; but the parables do not attack them. In Jesus' time there were prostitutes; but the parables do not heap on them the contempt that society felt for them. Surprisingly, Jesus' parables are not directed against the sins of the irreligious, but rather against the sins of the religious, and particularly against their refusal to see the inbreaking of the Kingdom. When we realize this and reassign the cast of characters, particularly if we do it on the basis of the question of power and powerlessness, the parables may take on a very different meaning, which may be closer to the original.

This is true of the entire Bible, both as a whole and in its various parts. Since liberation theologians see the Bible as above all a book of history—the history of God's liberating acts—the point at which we identify with that history is of crucial importance.

Let us look again at the story of Simon Magus in Acts 8, to which we referred earlier, and see how the text looks as we assign the cast of characters in different ways. Our normal reaction is to think that Simon Magus is whoever is opposing the church, or whoever is teaching incorrect doctrine.

As a matter of fact, since a very early date in the history of the church Simon Magus has become an ecclesiastical scapegoat. In the ancient church, he was the reputed father of all heresies. In the Middle Ages, the practice of buying and selling ecclesiastical offices was dubbed "simony," after Simon Magus. This means that we identify immediately with the hero of the story, Simon Peter, and place our enemies in the role of Simon Magus.

There are other characters with whom we could identify or that we should at least try on for size. One of these is Philip, who apparently received Simon Magus into the church without asking too many questions. Do we not allow ourselves to be overwhelmed by the prestige of the powerful, to the point that we are hesitant to ask of them the proper questions? Has not the church throughout its history received many a potentate and given them authority within the Christian community, without forcing them to face up to the radical demands of the gospel? Do we not assume that a lawyer or professor who joins the congregation should be given a prominent role very quickly? When we assign ourselves to the role of Philip, the entire story takes on a different meaning.

But then, should we not look also at the possibility that we may be in a position similar to that of Simon Magus? If at this point we ask the question of power and powerlessness, it may well be that, at least in the context of the distribution of wealth throughout the world, we are in the position of Simon Magus. Our North American society and the church which is a part of it have grown accustomed to having all be amazed at our power. When we read the text in this light, it tells us that we must beware of the Philips who are willing to preach the message to us, without showing us that to accept that message means to accept an entirely different ordering of power, and that we must be willing to hear the word of God as it comes to us through the Simon Peters of today's world—the fisherfolk on a lake in Nicaragua, the political prisoners in various countries, the women whose rights are trampled.

At this point the reader may wish to choose a narrative passage in Scripture and see what are the various ways in which a cast of characters can be assigned. Take, for instance, II Kings 6:8-28. Again, we may be tempted to identify with the prophet Elisha, who knows the plans of the enemy before they execute them, and who can see the invisible hosts of the Lord. Try putting yourself (and your congregation) in the place of the servant who sees only the armies of the enemy and for whose enlightenment Elisha prays. In what sense is this a better point of identification? What political realities, both in the text and in today's situations, would seem to make one or the other of these points of identification more adequate? And, once we have identified our own role, who among our contemporaries plays the other roles?

This perspective-taking, however, must not be used as an excuse for allegorizing, about which we shall have more to say later on. Allegorizing avoids the concrete, political setting of the text and of its hearers. This is the opposite. Take into account the setting in both the text and the contemporary situation before you decide on an assignment of roles. All interpretation assumes a placement, but often this is done quite unconsciously and reflects where we stand in society. This subconscious placement in the text is part of the received tradition. In a summer school course at Perkins School of Theology some years ago, we asked a group of students to list some of the passages that had meant the most to them. Interestingly enough, a large number of them chose Luke 4:18-19, where Jesus reads and applies to himself the words of Isaiah: "The Spirit of the Lord is upon me. . . ." Most interesting, however, was that white males chose this passage and invariably interpreted it as referring to their call to ministry. The Spirit of the Lord had anointed them to preach good news to the poor, etc. But those among the women and the minority men who chose the same text interpreted it quite differently. Most important to them was that Jesus had been anointed to bring good news to them, to proclaim release to them, etc. In short, those who were used to being in positions of privilege identified at one place, while those whose experience was the opposite identified at another.

A preacher who has ideological suspicion soon comes to ask the question of the cast of characters almost automatically, and then comes to the realization that this sort of question must be asked, not only of particular texts, but also of the entire thrust of biblical history. Why is it that in Christian communities even the most powerful think that they stand with the children of Israel and do not see that in many ways they are closer to Pharaoh than to Moses and his host? Why is it that so many preachers, when approaching a prophetic text, take for granted that they are the prophets, and the congregation is the disobedient Israel that must be chastised? Why is it that so many secure, prosperous congregations can read the psalms that deal with powerlessness or with political persecution as if they were the powerless and the persecuted? Why is it that so many religious folk can listen to the teachings of Jesus as if they were the despised publicans and harlots who will go first into God's Reign? If the question of power and powerlessness is fundamental in order to understand the message of Scripture, the manner in which that question may be brought home to us is through the way in which we assign the characters in the biblical account.

Imagine a Different Setting

Another manner in which a preacher can gain new insight into the meaning of a text is to imagine it being studied and expounded in a different socio-political setting. Some examples should clarify what this means. Take for instance the 23rd Psalm. We all know that psalm by heart, and we know exactly in what sort of setting to use it. Because it speaks of the "valley of the shadow of death," and because of its generally comforting character, we read it at funerals. Because of the shepherding and bucolic imagery of the first verses, we read it when we feel harassed and anxious. And there is no doubt that there is much in the psalm that commends this usage. But the preacher who intends to preach on this psalm will profit by imagining it set in different circumstances. Imagine, for instance, this psalm being read in an underground church in Nazi Germany, in the context of a communion service. In that scenario what stands out is not only the valley of the shadow of death, but also the table prepared in the presence of the enemies—an image that is hardly appropriate at a funeral, and that is therefore usually glossed over. But then change the setting and imagine this psalm being read by a group of Christians in a slum in the Dominican Republic, who are hungry because a North American company has taken over their land in order to plant sugar cane, and who have been forced to move to the slums in the capital. At that point, the table in the psalm becomes an expression that God will indeed fill a very real need. It becomes impossible to read the psalm as if there were no reference to food in it. And immediately the next step is taken: the "enemies" become very real. Many Western, affluent Christians are embarrassed by the reference to the enemies in that psalm. Many a sermon in such affluent settings either glosses over the "enemies" or interprets them allegorically as temptations or death itself. But our hungry Dominican sisters and brothers will not see the text in that fashion. They are really hungry. They are hungry because they have enemies—perhaps not enemies who hate them, but nevertheless enemies who are destroying them. To them, a very significant part of the promise of the psalm is that they shall be fed, and that such feeding will also be a vindication before their enemies. Given the situation of today's world, we may be the enemy to whom they are referring.

Given the current globalization of the economy, the hungry "enemies" may be closer to home. Suppose for instance that factory is being closed and moved overseas, so that profits may be increased. The tendency then will be to pit the interests of the US employees against their overseas counterparts. But in truth, if we are executives or shareholders in that company, or a government official that offers a deal, and if our decision has been made mainly for our profit, we shall be the enemies of those who will lose their jobs. Thus, imagining the psalm being read and interpreted in a different setting will lead the preacher to assign the cast of characters in a very different way than would be the case without such an exercise. In fact, it may be helpful to use more than one placement in a single sermon, in order to help different members of the congregation to relate to the text from their own situation.

By applying this methodology the preacher seeks to restore the text to its original setting, or at least to one that is politically similar to it. Very often a text is made more oppressive by reading it in a setting that is very different from the original one. This is the case with the three passages of the New Testament dealing with household legislation: Eph. 5:21-6:9; Col. 3:18-4:1; I Peter 2:18-3:7. There are women who study God's will for them, and who take as their point of departure what these texts say about the submissive role of wives. But in reading these texts alone or only in groups of women, they are missing what was also part of the original text and its situation, that is, that at the same time that the wives were listening to these words they were also overhearing the words addressed to husbands, which clearly limited the use of their power.

In a similar manner, these texts were used a few generations ago in order to instill in slaves a spirit of acceptance of their condition. But in such cases what very often took place was that the slaves were read only the words addressed to them, and not those directed at the masters, who are told, for instance, to "do the same to them" (Eph. 6:9). In some places there are still churches standing where the slave gallery had a high wall in front of it, allowing the slaves to see only the altar and the pulpit, but not their masters. The reason for this was that a slave-owning society was keenly aware of the need to avoid having the slaves see their masters kneeling! But in the early church the slaves did see the masters—or at least any such as were present— kneeling. The words of the New Testament, intended to be read and applied in such socially mixed company, came to have a different meaning when read in a setting which was intentionally segregated between masters and slaves—or, in our day, between males and females.

Because the Lone-Ranger Bible study is out, the preacher can enlist the help of others in the congregation, or outside of it, in this process of imagining a different setting. For instance, the male preacher can gain insight from the manner in which the women of his congregation, particularly those who are aware of the need for a new interpretation of the Bible, understand a particular text. Very few male interpreters would have been aware of the manner in which Jesus rejected the stereotype of woman as wife and mother in the two texts discussed in the last chapter. But this might soon have surfaced in a group of women applying their experience and their responses to the study of the Bible.

This definitely does not mean that the preacher will then proceed to preach on the meaning of the text in another setting. To do so would be to deny the basic principle that theology must always be concrete. To preach in Atlanta, Georgia, to a white middle-class congregation, a sermon about the meaning of the 23rd Psalm for the hungry in the slums of the Dominican Republic may be very enlightening about the conditions of hunger in that country, and how such conditions deny the worth of the human creature; but it will not be relating the text to this congregation. What the preacher will do in this case is to take note of the insights gained by placing the text in the context of hunger in the Dominican Republic and then return to the concrete situation of a particular congregation in Atlanta, in order to see what the text has to say here. Why does the Atlanta congregation—and the Atlanta preacher, apart from this exercise—fail to see in the text what is so evident in the Dominican Republic? Investigating that failure, the preacher in Atlanta may see a sign of the nature of the oppression under which the North American congregation lives. Its oppression will undoubtedly be of a different degree and quality from that of the Dominican peasant. But still, it is that oppression, and the manner in which it conspires with the much greater oppression of the Dominican peasant, that must be addressed in Atlanta. Otherwise we are still at the rather innocuous level of the do-gooder liberal preacher.

Consider the Direction of the Action

There are many portions of the Bible which have repeatedly caused difficulties for interpreters. Even before the advent of Christianity, there were difficulties in Judaism regarding various laws that seemed terribly crass to the cultured Hellenistic mind. The solution found by many was to interpret Scripture allegorically. Such allegorical interpretation, however, is less than useless. By determining what different elements in the biblical narrative or in the laws mean, the interpreter ends up determining what is to be found in Scripture—very much like the magician who surreptitiously places a rabbit inside a hat, and then pulls it out in public with much fanfare. The net result of such a procedure is that the Bible comes to naught, and what is actually preached and taught is the opinion of the person who determines what the symbols mean.

But having said that, we must still deal with the many passages of Scripture whose relevance for today is difficult to see. There are laws about slavery, the injunction that women must cover their heads when they preach, with the counterpart that a man's head remain uncovered, the seemingly contradictory order that women are to keep silent in the church, the instruction that younger widows are to remarry, have children, and keep house, and many others.

The usual way in which liberal interpreters dispose of such difficulties is to declare that they simply reflect the culture of the time when the Bible was written. One problem with this explanation is that very often such interpreters ignore the passages that would seem to contradict their understanding of the culture surrounding the Bible. For instance, in Luke 8:1-3 we see that among those who traveled from place to place with Jesus were a number of women, and that these women were the ones who covered the expenses of the entire group. This passage, which paints a very different picture than the more usual of Jesus and the twelve going from place to place and living on alms, is often ignored by liberal interpreters, for it does not fit their under-standing of the culture of the times, and of how Christianity related to that culture.

But there are other reasons why it will not do simply to say that passages having to do with subjects such as slavery and the subjection of women are "culturally determined." It will not do, first of all, because it is a truism which can be universally applied. There is no doubt that the culture of the times can be seen in these passages. But there is also no doubt that it can be seen in every single portion of the Bible, from the first chapter of Genesis to the last of Revelation, including such beloved texts as the parables of Jesus and John 3:16. Secondly, this explanation will not do because it places twentieth century culture in the privileged position of being able to decide what in the biblical past was culturally determined and what was not. The Bible never says: "This is culturally determined and therefore can be ignored." Nor does it say about other passages: "This is absolute, eternal, immutable truth, which is valid in every cultural setting." Finally, such a solution, precisely because it makes our culture the ultimate judge as to which portions of the Bible are still valid, and which are not, eventually means that the Bible no longer has a word from outside, and we are simply left with the usual type of theology, which does little more than reflect the present situation and ultimately works in favor of the status quo.

The manner in which liberation theology approaches this situation—and indeed the entire Bible—is by insisting on the historical character of revela-tion. Truth in the Bible is understood in a very different manner than it is sought by the philosophers who look for immutable essences. Truth in the Bible is God active in history. In consequence, what we must seek in Scripture is not immutable essences, nor eternal laws, but rather the record of God's action in history. And this action does not take place in some special domain of "salvation history"—what the Germans call *Heilsgeschichte*—but in the very history of which we and all humankind are a part.

Ignacio Ellacuría, one of the Jesuits martyred in El Salvador, ably stated what this means for our understanding of revelation:

> Now the communication of a living God in history means that this communication must be concerned with the history of human beings and that it must be so in a changing and progressive way. The two statements are interrelated. Without God's irruption into history, without his pres-ence in the historical realm, we would know very little about him. But if his presence is to be found in the historical realm, then we must be open to the changing irruption which is history.[5]

What this means is that, when reading a text in Scripture, we are not to see it as a gem floating in a void, but rather place it in its historical setting and ask the question of the direction of God's action in that text. Then, and only then, can we seek to apply the text to our own time.

Since several of the examples quoted above have to do with either slavery or the place of women in the church and in society, it may be well to show what this principle means by applying it to a passage which deals with slaves and with women, and to which we have had occasion to refer already.

Ephesians 5:21–6:9 is the most detailed of the three main texts in the New Testament dealing with "household legislation." This text is usually interpreted in one of two ways. Some take it to be absolute, immutable law and on that basis claim that the submission of wives to husbands is part of the changeless will of God. Others say that what we have here is an expression of the culture of the times, and therefore ought to be disregarded. The first position is hardly tenable when, as we have suggested earlier, the instructions regarding slaves and masters are seen as an integral part of the passage. To say that this text proves that the submission of wives to their husbands is part of the immutable will of God would immediately imply that the same is true of slavery. The second position is tempting, for it would allow us to do away with the uncomfortable passage about slaves. But then one would still be left with the question of whether or not wives ought to submit to their husbands. And the answer to that question would depend, not on the text itself, but on the interpreter's decision as to whether that particular injunction is an expression of the culture of the times or of the immutable will of God. Along these lines of debate, the biblical text itself soon loses all relevance.

Liberation theology would lead to interpreting this text— as well as any other—along historical lines. In other words, the interpreter looks at the concrete situation in which these words were written, sees in what direction they point given that situation, and then follows the same direction in today's world.

In the case of the text in question, what we must first ask is what was the situation of wives, children, and slaves at the time of this writing. Obviously, this presents some difficulties in this particular case, for scholars are not agreed as to the date of authorship of this document, nor as to who were its intended readers—the words "in Ephesus" in 1:1 do not appear in a number of important manuscripts. But in any case it seems likely that this document was written sometime in the second half of the first century, and that its context is the Eastern portion of the Empire—probably around Asia Minor.

The institution of marriage had been changing in the last years of the Roman Republic and the beginning of the Empire.[6] But these changes had taken place mostly in the West. In the East, the ancient Greek customs regarding marriage still held sway, often supported by a stricter interpretation of Roman law than was current even in Rome. In the Greek tradition, marriage was a very unequal relationship. For instance, men were allowed to have concubines, but if a woman committed adultery her husband was expected at least to divorce her, and both custom and law allowed him to kill her. Also women were confined to their own homes, and even there they were expected to remain in the section reserved for them, where very few males ever entered. Although in the western portion of the Roman Empire things had begun to change, in the East the conservatism of the region found support in the older laws. According to the ancient power of *manus*, the chief of a family had absolute authority over his own wife—and those of his sons. He could punish her disobedience even by death or by selling her into slavery. And her status was so low that she had no legal standing, to the point that her husband was legally responsible for her actions. In one kind of marriage, the contract took the form of a sale with the groom's father—or the groom himself, if he was a free agent—sealing the contract with a down payment. On such occasions, the groom gave his bride a ring as a symbol of the purchase price. By the first century, there were some limitations put on the power of a husband over his wife. For instance, in order to encourage population growth, Augustus decreed that any matron with three or more children would be granted a number of legal rights. But such a law, which saw women as reproductive machines, can hardly be said to have been a great advance toward a more balanced situation in marriage. In any case, in spite of the changing laws, the basic institution of marriage still saw the wife as a property and ward of her husband, and any laws protecting her were mere reflections of the laws protecting children—for instance, a great advancement was made when wives were allowed to inherit their husbands' estates on the same basis as did minor children.

The relationship between fathers and their children was similar to that between husbands and wives. (The NRSV correctly translates Ephesians 6:1 as "parents," and Ephesians 6:4 as "fathers.") When we read the text in Ephesians, and others like it, we take for granted that "children" here refers to minors. But such would not necessarily be the case at that time. According to Roman law, the oldest male member of the family, the *pater familias*, had the right of *manus* over all his children for life. A father had the right to determine whether a newly born child would be allowed to live or not. In the early years of the Christian church, it was still customary for poor children to be exposed—that is, left out to die—by their fathers, who did not have the means to support them. And rich fathers often decided to expose their sons—or grandsons—in order not to divide the inheritance. Even after it was decided that the child would live, the *pater familias* had the right to kill or sell it. That right was seldom exercised, and there were attempts to limit it by law. But as late as the fourth century it still existed.

Likewise, a son could hold no property as long as his father lived—a daughter's case was somewhat different, for on her marriage she came under the jurisdiction of her husband's *pater familias*. Any money the son made, even if he was a high government official or a general, belonged to his father. The same was true of all legal rights, which were vested in the father for as long as they both lived.

Besides the death of the *pater familias*, there was one other way in which a son could be freed from such a dependent situation. That was a legal process called "emancipation." To do this, a father had to sell his son to a friend, who then returned him. After doing this three times, the father could declare the son "emancipated." But even then the son was not entirely free, for he now stood in a relationship to his father similar to that of a freed slave and the former master.

The condition of slaves was obviously worse. A slave had no rights and could be shamed, tortured, or killed at the master's whim. A slave's word had no standing in court, unless the deposition had been obtained through the use of torture. An untractable slave was often put to death, usually by crucifixion. If any dared raise their hand against their master, not only the guilty party, but any other slaves who happened to be under the same roof at the time were condemned to death. Often elderly slaves were expelled from the household to die of hunger.

Like a child, a slave could be freed. Some slaves were able to save enough money to buy their own freedom. Others were manumitted—set free—by their masters. In ancient Rome, a slave could be manumitted simply by being invited to sit at the master's table. But Imperial Rome wished to preserve the institution of slavery and took steps to make manumission much more difficult. The number of slaves that could be set free at one time was curtailed. And Augustus decreed that no slave under thirty could be set free, except in the case of extraordinary service—such as saving the master's life—which had to be proven before the law. (This may be a point to take into consideration when studying the Epistle to Philemon, for if Onesimus was under thirty there was no way in which his master could legally set him free.) Older slaves could buy their freedom by paying their masters with their own savings. But this was possible only if the master permitted it, for legally those savings also belonged to the *pater familias*.

Even freed slaves did not have the status of free citizens. They still remained in a special relationship of dependency to their former masters. If a freed slave died without leaving children, the inheritance went to the former master—the *patronus*. And in any case the freed slave had a number of obligations toward the *patronus*, which had to be fulfilled under penalty of being sold back into slavery.

Such were the conditions that obtained at the time of the writing of the Epistle to the Ephesians. One half of each of the three pairs mentioned—wives, children, slaves—had practically no rights, while the other half—husbands, fathers, masters—had all the rights and the power. When we then read the passage in question with this background in mind, we find that what stands out is not the words to the powerless, because their relationship to the powerful was taken for granted. Indeed, to have said anything else would have made the document and its author, as well as any church which read it in its gatherings, liable to prosecution for sedition and disregard for the law. So, the author stays within the bounds of the law in telling wives, children, and slaves to fulfill their obligations.

But then come the words to the powerful. What in essence such words say is that the powerful ought not to abuse their power, and that the reason for this is that there is Another more powerful than they, who demands just treatment for the powerless. Thus, the husbands are clearly reminded that they are part of the bride of Christ, that is, that they too have a husband. And the masters are reminded that they too have a master. On this basis, husbands and wives, fathers and children, masters and slaves are to "be subject to one another out of reverence for Christ" (5:21), and masters are to act toward slaves in the same way that slaves are required to act toward them (6:8).

These words were intended to be read, not to slaves, children and wives in one meeting and then to masters, fathers, and husbands in another meeting, but to all together. Short of actual sedition, it is hard to imagine what more revolutionary words could be written at that time!

All of this clarifies for us the *direction* of the text. And it is that direction that is all important. At that particular time in history, these words were subverting the established order of inequality and injustice. They were doing so by the demand that the powerful limit their power. At the time, strengthening the power of the weak was not an option. Either form—or both together—alter the situation toward justice. To use them to uphold today whatever remains of such injustice in family relations would be to use them in a direction absolutely contrary to their intention. What we must do is exactly the opposite. These words invite us to examine our contemporary relationships, see what in them is unjust, and be certain that God's will opposes such injustice.

In conclusion, in interpreting any text a preacher should avoid taking it as concrete and immutable instructions for every situation, but rather inquire after the direction of the action in its original setting and then seek to act, and to invite others to act, in the same direction.

Avoid Avoidance

There is a very human tendency to avoid portions of Scripture that do not make sense to us or that appear to contradict what we understand the gospel to be about. If the truth be known, many preachers decide on a sermon, and then look for a text to go with it, undisturbed by the fact that parts of the chosen text are irrelevant or even contradict what the sermon **says.** The increasing use of a lectionary does overcome this tendency to a large degree, because the preacher begins with the text rather than with the sermon.

Even so, when a biblical passage is looked at with the clear task of preaching in mind, there is always a first reaction. It may be one of immediate pleasure—that one can easily imagine how to deal with the text. This is often a problem, however, because the preacher may go off on a theme that the text presents and then really ignore the specificity of the passage itself. There can also be the initial reaction that we have no idea at all what to do. The text is strange. We don't like it. Such an initial reaction may make us leave the passage quickly and go on to one we can figure out easily.   If we have become hermeneutically suspicious, however, our reaction may be quite different. We may distrust the sense that we know what a passage means when we first see it. What we think it says is probably part of the received tradition we need to look at. And when we discover a text that really seems strange —or even unpleasant—we may find it important to work with it, to see what is actually happening in the passage and what it says to us in our situation.

Quite often, the most significant discoveries in a text come when we pay attention to details which the more traditional interpretations ignore. As Walter Brueggemann says,

> The parts of the Bible that "do not fit" credal theology or rational criticism may turn out to be the most important. The text voices what ill fits and often offers it to us in the form of details, but we do not sufficiently linger over those details. A good exegete, like a good therapist, will linger over precise wording, the odd incongruity, the repeated accent, in order to notice what commonly remains unnoticed.[7]

A good example is II Corinthians 8:7-15, a passage which occurs in the lectionary. It has to do with the collection for the Jerusalem church. The reasoning becomes a little convoluted and concludes with a quotation: "The one who had much did not have too much, and the one who had little did not have too little." The preacher might readily decide that it would be simple to deal with the theme of generosity, or with the statement about Jesus having become poor for our sake, or that we should show the genuineness of our faith by our actions. Any or all of these could be done without trying to figure out that cryptic statement at the end.

However, if one's curiosity were piqued by that strange verse, one would discover it comes from Exodus 16:18, in the account of the manna. If we were to ask a group of Christians what were the miracles concerning the manna, they would probably remember that God provided food for the people. Then, if pushed, they might remember that it spoiled if they tried to keep it from one day to the next, except for the day before the Sabbath. That is probably all that we were taught about it. But that is not the whole story in Exodus, as this verse indicates. According to Exodus 16, the head of each tent or household was to collect an omer—about a quart—of manna for each person in the tent. As is typical in human societies, some gathered too much, and others did not get enough. But then it was measured, and a miracle had occurred: those who had gathered too much had just the right amount; and those who had not gotten enough, had exactly what their portion should have been. Why is it that most often sermons revolve around God providing the manna, and not about God distributing it justly among the people? What does that have to say about the selective character of the tradition as we have received it? Could it be that we dwell on one miracle, rather than the other, because as a society we can boast of imitating God the provider, but not God the distributor?

What does this have to say about the collection for the church in Jerusalem? When quoting this passage, Paul is not anticipating another miracle that will come in and redistribute the excess from Corinth so that Jerusalem will have enough. He seems to assume that those who are part of the same Body of Christ will do this themselves. What does that say about our life as a church across all sorts of political and economic dividing lines?

There are other kinds of surprises in texts. Several years ago, when it became fashionable to hold ecumenical services in which important dignitaries represented their denominations, Justo was asked to read the Scripture at one such service. There were a Catholic archbishop and two Protestant bishops present, as well as several other dignitaries, all in full garb. Not to appear much less, I was wearing academic regalia. The reading, as could be expected, was the famous passage on the Body of Christ in I Corinthians 12:12-27. That was no surprise. I read: "Just as the body is one and has many members. . . ." No surprise there. "If the whole body were an eye, where would the ear be?" Still, no surprise. "There are many members, yet one body. . . . " We have all heard than before. But then, looking at myself and at those sharing the platform with me, I could hardly keep a straight face: "And those members of the body that we think are less honorable we clothe with greater honor, and our less respectable members are treated with greater respect"!

These two verses, 22-25, are often skipped in the reading of this passage. Or, when they are not skipped, we read them quickly, perhaps hoping no one will notice. We certainly do not preach about them. We are quite comfortable speaking about the eyes and ears, the feet and the hands. But when we come to the "less honorable parts of the body" we decide this would not be appropriate for a sermon. Yet to avoid these verses is really to ignore the heart of what Paul is saying. Paul is not simply speaking the commonly known, that in any society different people have different functions. He is speaking about this particular community, the church, and he is addressing the specific church in Corinth, where some people think that they are more important than the rest, and where apparently those who can bring abundant food to the love feast gorge themselves, while others go hungry. And he is telling them that in this particular body, the church, those who would otherwise be deemed less honorable must be clothed with greater honor. In a way, these verses that we ignore or slur are at the very core of the message of the Epistle. Why do we avoid them? Probably for two concomitant reasons: first, we are not comfortable speaking of the "shameful parts of the body"; second and most important, we are not ready to model our own church life after the teachings of Paul on this point. On the other hand, by focusing our attention on that which is usually avoided, we gain greater insight, not only into this particular passage, but also into the entire Epistle.

A final example may be in order. When we hear the phrase, "the sign of Jonah," we immediately think of the time that Jonah spent in the belly of the monster, and its parallelism with the time that Jesus spent in the grave. The basis for this is found in Matthew 12:40, where Jesus explicitly establishes that parallelism. Significantly, however, that is not all that he says, for he continues: "The people of Nineveh will rise up at the judgment with this generation and condemn it, because they repented at the proclamation of Jonah, and see, something greater than Jonah is here!" (Matt. 12:41).

The parallel text in Luke 11:29-30 does not even mention the three days and three nights in the belly of the monster, but speaks only of the people of Nineveh. Both texts, in Matthew and in Luke, then go on to speak of "the queen of the South" as a sign. The point then is that, just as in Jonah's time and also in the case of the queen of the South, the unlikely will come in.

Why then do we take for granted that "the sign of Jonah" refers to the three days and nights, and forget that is also (and even primarily) refers to the conversion and repentance of the irreligious? Could it be because we, like Jonah, secretly wish to reserve the goodness of God for ourselves, and would much rather not share it with those whom we despise?[8]

In this case, in traditional interpretation we avoid the reference to the people of Nineveh and to the queen of the South. By avoiding such avoidance, we gain new insight both into the text and into the hidden agendas which have led to traditional interpretations. Thus, a final "pointer" in this chapter is to look precisely at that which is ignored or left aside, for there may be the clue to a different, richer, and more liberating interpretation of the text.

V

Making Connections

For the last several centuries, the church as we know it has managed to separate three elements that the ancient church held together. We are able to discuss Scripture, preaching, and liturgy as quite separate topics. Obviously there are connections. We know that preaching ought to have some clear relationship to Scripture. We assume that most preaching takes place within the context of public worship. (Evangelistic preaching takes place outside the worshiping congregation, but here we are concerned basically with preaching that is addressed to the faithful who are gathered.) But Scripture, preaching, and liturgy are clearly separable elements—so separable, that in the medieval period there could be liturgy without preaching, and in many Protestant churches in the nineteenth century, liturgy was hardly the term appropriate for the opening and closing exercises that surrounded the main event of the sermon. Even with the clearly liturgical moments of the sacraments, in many cases baptism is a parenthesis in a service that goes on as though the baptism had not taken place, and the Lord's Supper is an occasional appendix to an otherwise unchanged worship service. We have all heard sermons in which the link with Scripture was tangential at best—and at worst, no need was seen at all to connect the two.

For the early church, on the other hand, it was a very different matter. There was no printing press. Christians did not have private copies of the Bible. One usually had to hear Scripture read—and that meant gathering in worship. The liturgy, the Scripture, its explanation and application—all were combined in a single series of events, at a single place. When Paul's letters were read the most ancient church, were they viewed as Scripture? As sermon to this congregation? As part of the worship service? As all three combined? As a mix of the three, not yet defined?

We stand in a very different place. Surely we should not give up the printed Bibles we take for granted, or the electronic versions that we will soon accept as normal. But it may indeed be helpful to recapture the unity of these elements—or at least to see the connections among them. For the early church, Scripture was indeed a powerful, liberating force. Could it have been such without the other two elements? Could preaching have had its force without liturgy? Could the liturgy have been so transforming without a particular view of Scripture?

Traditions of Biblical Interpretation

As we look at the early history of the church, at least as it is portrayed in the first chapters of the book of Acts, it appears that the struggle of the emerging Christian community with the religious establishment is, at least in part, a struggle over the possession of Scripture—the possession, not of the book itself, but of the history which the book portrays. This is certainly the issue in Stephen's speech before the Sanhedrin, which takes up fully 5 percent of the entire book of Acts. The Just One whom you have rejected, says Stephen, was announced and typified by Moses, who was also rejected by his fellow Israelites when he killed the Egyptian, and was rejected again in the desert, when they made the golden calf. (In Stephen's speech, the same is true, before Moses, of Joseph, who was sold into slavery by his brothers, as well as of the many prophets who came after Moses and who were also persecuted.) And, just as Moses was made ruler and liberator of the people, so has this Jesus now been raised to the right hand of God. Who, then, is blaspheming against Moses?, says Stephen. We who like him are rejected because we announce One who like him was rejected? Or you, the powerful of Israel, who like Joseph's brothers gave up the Just One in order to save your power? Who uses the Scriptures correctly, you who use them to persecute us, as the prophets were persecuted before, or we who, like those prophets, announce the astonishing actions of God?

The earliest Christian theology developed in the midst of a community that was not of great account in the eyes the world. The social status of early Christians may be open to debate; but certainly, by the very fact that they were Christians if not also by reason of their social origins, Christians were a despised lot.[1]

In such a situation, the early church drew great strength and comfort from a view of history which both promised a different future and made sense of the sufferings and humiliations of the present. Joseph sold by his brothers, yet made a ruler in Egypt; Moses rejected by his own people, yet

97

raised to be their deliverer; the stone which the builders rejected, but which was then made the cornerstone of the building; all these were pre-enactments of the great drama of history, in which Jesus, the new Moses, the stone rejected by the builders of Israel, was crucified, yet risen again to rule in glory. And the same was true of Christians themselves, who like Joseph, like Moses, but above all like Christ, were the rejected stones of society. In Scripture those early Christians found the power to resist the oppressive structures that would silence them.

In the next chapter in Acts after Stephen's speech, we find Philip speaking to the Ethiopian eunuch. As was mentioned before, here is a man condemned by the law of Scripture to remain forever an outsider, for the law clearly states that a eunuch cannot be added to the people of God. A pathetic picture. The man has come to Jerusalem to worship; but the law of the God whom he worships excludes him (Deut. 23:1). But Philip and the eunuch engage in a conversation, as the text says, "beginning with this scripture"—that is, with Isaiah 53. Did they continue reading Isaiah as far as the 56th chapter? It is impossible to tell. If they did, they would have read the promise of God: "To the eunuchs who keep my sabbaths, who choose the things that please me and hold fast to my covenant, I will give in my house and within my wall a monument and a name better than sons and daughters; I will give them an everlasting name which shall not be cut off."

Whatever Scripture Philip used, Acts says that "beginning with this scripture he told him the good news of Jesus." What is the good news? That in Jesus the promises have been fulfilled, that the Reign of God, the time promised by the prophets, has been inaugurated. And so, when they come to a place where there is water, the eunuch says, "See, there is water! What is to prevent my being baptized?" According to the traditional use of Scripture, the answer was clear: Deuteronomy 23:1. But according to Philip's use of Scripture, in light of the good news of Jesus, the answer is, "nothing," and they descended into the water, and Philip baptized the eunuch.

Other examples could be adduced, both from the New Testament itself and from patristic literature; but the point is that the early church has a way of reading Scripture that is liberating, not only against the powers from outside that would oppress it, but even from an understanding of Scripture itself that could be used to oppress and stifle it.

Do we today have that sense of the liberating power of Scripture? Certainly, there are many Christians in our day who do have such a sense. A few years ago, we went to Central America with a group of students. They were astonished by the sense of hope that these Christians had, even in the midst of terrible circumstances. Other students remained in Atlanta, in a housing project in the city. For them, there was a sense of hopelessness that permeated lives there. For many Christians in difficult situations there is hope. Yet for many of us, and certainly for many in the churches which we serve and where we worship, this sense has been lost.

In the Western church, both Protestant and Roman Catholic, traditionally the most common ways to read Scripture have been as law and as prophecy. As law, Scripture tells us what to do. This is related to an entire theological outlook in which God is seen as legislator and judge, sin as breaking the law, and redemption as paying the penalty for sin. From this perspective, the Bible is read as a rule book to tell us what we ought to do in a given situation.

There are many problems with this approach to Scripture. One of the most serious is that it fragments the Bible. Instead of a coherent whole, with its own movement and direction, it becomes a series of practically independent rules. Which rule applies? one asks when approaching the Bible, very much as a lawyer asks when approaching a case—and it is no coincidence that the technical term for this kind of interpretation is "casuistry," nor that casuistry has also developed all the negative connotations with which we are familiar. Even at its best, casuistry sees moral decision and even religious life as a series of "cases" with very little connection to each other, except where the same legal principles apply.

Another negative consequence of this approach is that most of Scripture can be ignored. It can be ignored in any particular instance, once the appropriate law that applies has been determined, and it can be ignored in general, for most of Scripture is not legal in nature.

A second approach that has become quite common in Western tradition is prophecy. When this word is employed in everyday language, even in the church, what is meant is that the words of Scripture somehow announce something that will happen in the future. From this perspective, the significance of the Old Testament lies mostly in that it includes the writings of prophets who foretold the coming of Jesus, and the significance of at least certain books of the New Testament is that they foretell what will happen in the future or, even more frequently in our day, what is happening right now.

As with the legal approach, the main difficulty with this approach is that it effectively discounts most of Scripture, for even in the books of Isaiah and Micah, there are no more than a few words or passages that can be seen as prophetic in the sense of foretelling the future.

A second difficulty is obviously that it renders even such prophetic passages practically meaningless until they have been fulfilled, and valueless once they have been fulfilled. If Isaiah 53, for instance, is a literal prophecy referring specifically and only to the sufferings of Jesus, then it meant nothing to those who read it before the time of Jesus. And after that time, we no longer need it, for we have much more detailed descriptions of that suffering in the Gospels. Or, if the book of Revelation is a prophecy about our days, as some very popular books are saying, then it did not mean a thing

99

to Christians in the time of Augustine, or of Luther, except that some day our time would come.

Clearly, these two methods of interpretation existed in the early church and have continued throughout the history of the church. Yet, also clearly, they leave much to be desired.

It is for this reason that at a relatively early date a different approach became popular. This is allegorical interpretation. Throughout history, when Christian exegetes have not liked the limitations of the legal and the prophetic approach, they have often had resort to allegory. From this perspective, everything in Scripture has a hidden meaning, if only one can find it. This is precisely the value and the attraction of this method. If one does not know what to make of what Scripture says about pigs being unclean, one can always decide that what the text really means is that we are not to be like pigs, that remember their master only when they are hungry.

Or we can do like a student Justo once had who thought he was a great preacher. He was assigned to preach a sermon for Palm Sunday. As we all know, that is not an easy occasion on which to preach. But this student found a way out. He read that Jesus told the disciples to go untie the colt of the ass. From that point he took off. "We are all tied by our sins," he said, "and we need Jesus to untie us." All that he said was true. It just had nothing to do with the text. When he came down from the pulpit, proud of his eloquence and his creativity, I could no longer resist. "That was a very interesting sermon," I told him, "but, do you realize you have just made an ass of yourself?"

Quite clearly, the early church did interpret Scripture in terms of law and prophecy—even on occasion in allegorical terms. But all of this is subsumed under another form of interpretation which places history at its very heart. Each of these forms of interpretation, law, prophecy, and allegory, have one thing in common: they focus on words rather than events. The actual text is handled almost like a magical book, rather than the history of the community of faith. Over against this, the most common form of interpretation in the early church focuses on events and their patterns and connections —in other words, it focuses on history.

In Stephen's speech before the Sanhedrin, mentioned earlier, he is not saying that a list of prophecies have been or are being fulfilled. He is saying that he, the church, and the Sanhedrin stand within a history. This is a history which does not repeat itself, but in which certain patterns appear. If one is to interpret Scripture faithfully, it must be within the scope of that history: Joseph was sold by his brothers into slavery; Moses was betrayed by the Israelites whom he sought to save by killing the Egyptian; Jesus was betrayed and murdered by those whom he came to save. Yet Joseph was made a ruler in Egypt, and an instrument for the salvation of those who sold him. Moses was made ruler and deliverer of the people who would have delivered him to the Egyptians. And now Jesus sits at the right hand of God and offers salvation, even to those who betrayed and killed him. "His brothers sold Joseph into slavery; the Israelites betrayed Moses; the people persecuted the prophets; I know where I stand," says Stephen; "I know where the community that follows Jesus stands; and, as a consequence, I know also where the Sanhedrin stands."

This kind of interpretation is usually called "typological," for it speaks of events in the past as "types" or "figures" of events to come. We could as well call it "historical" in the strict sense, for what characterizes a historical perspective is precisely the conviction that, while events do not repeat themselves, and while each of them is significant in itself, there are also patterns which make the knowledge of the past helpful. Joseph sold by his brothers, Moses rejected by the Israelites, the prophets persecuted, are all "types" or figures of Jesus. And, because he is the culmination of history, because he is both the One to whom all these types pointed and the goal to which all of history moves, he is also the *archetype* from which the church must draw the pattern of its life.

This is also the manner in which Scripture interprets itself. When the prophet whom we now call Second Isaiah seeks for an interpretation of the exile and the return, he draws on the pattern of God opening the Red Sea, so that, just as God made a path in the sea, now God makes a way in the wilderness. Or when the earliest evangelist seeks to interpret the "evangelion," the "good news" of what has happened in Jesus Christ, he draws on the image of the return from exile, quoting the prophet, "a voice cries in the wilderness: Prepare the way of the Lord." The Lord who prepared a way in the Sea and in the desert, once again prepares the way; and the people who were pilgrims across the sea and across the desert will now again be pilgrims.

This typological form of biblical interpretation is one that we have generally lost in the Western church, though it is beginning to appear again. It takes seriously the history of the People of God within which these types continue to occur, linking together generations centuries apart. It also provides a way for us to see our present experience as a part of this ongoing history. In fact, the beauty of this method is that it allows the parallels of our setting and the biblical account to come through without an intervening translation into doctrine. It does not require academic training. It requires immersion in the biblical story and an awareness of contemporary structures of power.

At this point, it is clear that the oppressed know best how to see this dimension in Scripture. It has been said that if you wish to know how the welfare system really works, the best way is not to read the laws about it, nor to speak with those who administer it, but to speak to those who are on welfare—or who should be. Likewise, the best way to know what the Bible says within this history is not by the mediation of some high-sounding hermeneutical principle or methodology. One does not even need to seek to "apply" the text politically. It happens naturally, through those who in the midst of their oppression read in Scripture a story similar to theirs. They know the real structures of power better than the rest of society, just as those on welfare know that system best.

And it happens even implicitly, without the need to spell out what is meant. When the slaves on a plantation sang "Go down Moses," they knew what they were really singing. The master knew only that they were singing about the Bible. But they knew that they were singing about the Bible *and* about themselves. And they saw a unity between the two that probably remained hidden to the master.

Let us look briefly at one biblical narrative that has been a favorite with children: the account of David and Goliath in I Samuel 17. If most of us were asked to retell the story, we would probably remember that David was young, not yet old enough to be a soldier. He was sent by his father Jesse to take food to his older brothers who were in Israel's army, fighting under King Saul against the Philistines. When he got to the lines, David heard that the Philistine giant, Goliath, was taunting the army of Israel. No one in Israel would go to fight him. David, however, was sure that God would not let him be defeated. He therefore volunteered to go out after Goliath. He rejected Saul's offer of traditional armor, choosing to take only the slingshot with which he had defended his sheep from wild animals. With one shot he killed the great giant, and brought victory to Israel. The story is normally told so that the point for young Christians is quite clear: If you have faith in God, you can overcome any odds. It doesn't matter how small or how young you are. The narrative *can* be used in this way. David announced his faith. He is sure that it is God's strength and not his own that matters.

But to use the account in this way is to deal with it in an individualistic manner, and it also ignores the more complex history within which the story is set. From a typological perspective, one would deal with it quite differently.

First of all, we would need to determine where this text appears in the history of Israel. The place of David in that history makes a difference. David, like Moses, is treated as a type of Christ—whether in messianic prophecies looking for the one who is to come from the line of David, from the root of Jesse, or in the New Testament statements about Jesus who comes as this expected Davidic king. Furthermore, in the chapter before the account of Goliath, we read about Samuel, the prophet, who is commanded by God to go to the house of Jesse, to anoint the son of Jesse who had been chosen by God to be the new king of Israel. Samuel goes, and after seeing all seven of the mature sons of Jesse, discovers that God has not chosen any of them— but rather the unlikely youngest son, still a child, who is out tending the sheep. David is anointed by Samuel, but though anointed, still remains a shepherd, waiting until the time appointed by God when Saul shall no longer be king. Yet at the moment of the anointing, we are told that the Spirit of the Lord came mightily upon David—and also, that the same Spirit departed from Saul, even though he remained king.

Typologically, it is significant that it is not simply any youth, but the anointed one of God, upon whom God's Spirit has come, who has gone up against Goliath. It is a kingly act, in defense of his people, even though he is not yet the king. The parallels with Jesus would have been very obvious to those Christians in the early church who heard this story. Jesus is the Anointed One, the Christ, above all others. Like David, he was an unlikely candidate to be a king—born in a stable, not the sort of beginning one would expect for royalty! He was born in the little town of David, not in the city of Jerusalem. He too has been appointed king, yet in his lifetime he lived under another order, and was not yet publicly acclaimed as king. Jesus, like David, went out against the giants who defied the God of Israel—bigger giants than Goliath, giants of disease, of sin, of death, of all the powers of evil. He was a king, but with an anointing that had yet to be made public, even as David was when he went up against Goliath.

David won his battle with Goliath—and that is where we usually end the story for children. But typologically, one would continue far enough to see that this victory of David, great though it was, also brought him great trouble. For Saul began to be jealous of David from this point on. And Saul was still the ruling king. He would try to kill David. That would certainly be difficult to explain to children. Why would you want to be like David if the net result is that you make powerful enemies who try to kill you? But surely we see the full meaning of that in the life of Jesus. It is precisely his victories over sin, death, and evil—as seen for instance in the healing miracles—that cause the people to praise him and the leaders to seek to kill him. Being anointed by God brings both power over evil and the enmity of evil. Evil still reigns in this old order, though a new order, with a new king, has already begun.

Such an interpretation would mean that David is not simply an example that with faith in God, we can overcome all obstacles—true though that is. But David is also an example of the ambiguity of being God's anointed. Faith leads us into great danger, as well as giving us the ultimate power to conquer. Children need to know that as well. They need to see themselves as part of a community that lives out the danger as well as the victory that faith brings. The story would have even more significance if the children who heard it also knew that they had been anointed as part of their baptismal rite. In the early church, they would have known this. So the account would have come to them, not as a story of a young person, long ago, but as a story about themselves.

It was after the time of Constantine, early in the fourth century, that typology really lost ground. It lost ground precisely because the view of history which it espoused, and which looked forward to an end different than the glories of the Roman Empire, was not compatible with the growing alliance between Church and Empire. For over a millennium and a half, Christianity enjoyed respectability and the support of the state and of society at large. There was nothing strange or uncouth about being a Christian. On the contrary, all respectable people were Christians. Christians were no longer stones rejected by the master builders, but the builders who decided which stones to accept and which to reject. This may be seen in the efforts on the part of Eusebius of Caesarea to show that the conversion of Constantine was the goal towards which history had always been moving, and also in his doubts as to whether the book of Revelation, which spoke of a different view, should be included in the canon of the New Testament.[2]

It was in such a situation that typology lost ground, both in the East and in the West. In the East, it was not abandoned, but was rendered powerless in one of two ways. The first, of which Eusebius himself is a good example, was to limit history and its typology to past events. Eusebius himself interpreted the rise and reign of Constantine in terms of the typology of Moses, whom God had raised up to free the people. But then he refused to apply the same typology to current events, to those who in his own time were despised and persecuted. If the new King David had arrived in Constantine, it was not necessary to look beyond this kingdom to a greater one.

A second way in which typology lost power was by limiting it to purely ecclesiastical matters, and to those having to do with our eternal salvation. Like allegory, this new form of typology had little or nothing to do with history, but referred to eternal matters.

As long as the Constantinian arrangement lasted in the East, and even under hostile Muslim and Marxist regimes, such biblical interpretation was normative, and helped the church avoid many a conflict with the state.

In the West, the other two strains of biblical interpretation became normative. Indeed, to interpret Scripture as referring to a history in which the builders of society reject the stones chosen by God was a very questionable and even subversive thing. In contrast, allegorical interpretation, usually connected with heavenly realities of which we shall partake after death, reinforced a "pie in the sky" theology which led to quiet acceptance of present injustices, while the interpretation of Scripture as a book of law led to a sacralization of the present law and order which had similar social consequences.

The momentum has changed in recent decades. It began changing centuries ago, with the French Revolution and the rise of the secular state. But in recent decades, there have also been very significant developments. In 1900, roughly 50% of all Christians lived in Europe; by 1985, that number was reduced to 25%. In 1900, 80% of all Christians were white; by 1985, that figure was reduced to 40%. Most of these changes are due to the growing churches in the Third World, in areas that in 1940 were under colonial rule, but which are now independent. And most of the growth has taken place, not under colonial regimes that might have favored Christianity in a Constantinian style but after the end of colonial rule. In other words, in the midst of a post-Constantinian increasing secularism, these churches are growing and showing enormous vitality.

In the North Atlantic, the momentum has followed a different path. There has been growing secularism, joined with a decline in church membership and participation. In the United States, whatever the fluctuations in church membership in recent years, it is quite clear that in terms of our culture, we are becoming more and more secularized. A variety of activities are scheduled for Sunday mornings, from entertainment programs to children's soccer games. Church participation appears rarely in television dramas, except for funerals and weddings. Even in these brief appearances, the clergy often are quaint characters, out of touch with contemporary life. As a general rule, clergy do not have the social status they did a few generations ago. Many other professions have far greater prestige.

In Western Europe, the secularization process has proceeded at a more rapid pace. Participation in worship is infrequent, even for people who would identify themselves as Christians—and many would claim no such affiliation. In fact, it is not simply the growth of the church in areas outside of the old North Atlantic stronghold that has changed the statistics for the church worldwide—it is also the clear decline in percentages of population that would claim church membership within that traditional heart of medieval Christendom and the colonies it produced in North America. The development of communism in Russia and after World War II in Eastern Europe can be seen as a more rapid and pressured rise of secularism. Both Russia and Eastern Europe were taken abruptly from a strong Constantinian situation to a radically secular and clearly hostile social setting. Where typology had been used to sacralize the present order, it obviously would have to change—and to change in the direction of the ancient understandings.

In the last few years we have witnessed momentous events in what previously we called the communist block. After decades of pressure, persecution, and apparent non-existence, the church in China has shown itself to be still a vital force. The recent events in Russia and in Eastern Europe are well known. How have these churches survived? What has been the source of their strength? In one word, it has been their understanding of history, often kept alive by a liturgical life deeply grounded in that understanding.

Typology, Liturgy, and Identity

A liturgical revival is occuring throughout the Christian world. This renewal finds support in the early liturgies of the church, and owes much of its impetus to scholarly research and discoveries regarding those early liturgies. Indeed, we have learned that early Christian worship was very different than we—both Catholics and Protestants—had assumed. But the impetus behind this liturgical renewal is far from the purely scholarly or antiquarian. In Africa, Asia and Latin America, among minorities in the North Atlantic, and in a myriad other places, Christian communities are developing liturgies which in many ways approach what we know of the liturgies of the early church. Thus, while scholars in the North Atlantic have been researching the worship of the early church, Christians in various parts of the world have been developing patterns of worship which bear some of the characteristics of that early worship. Part of the reason is that, like the early church, many of these Christians cannot count on society to support their faith. And also like the early church, these Christians are finding support on a typological understanding of Scripture and of history.

A seminary professor who specializes in Eastern Orthodox theology tells the story of something that happened to him several years ago. He had taken a group from this country in a study tour of the Soviet Union. As is customary in such cases, a guide had been assigned to his group—a guide whose function was to be polite and helpful, but who was also clearly there as a representative of the Party and its interests. Because the group was composed mostly of seminary students and pastors, and because the purpose of the visit was to come to a greater understanding of the Russian Orthodox Church, they attended a number of liturgical celebrations. The guide made it quite clear that he was uncomfortable in such places, which according to him were no more than the remnants of a by-gone age. Yet as the days passed he grew more pensive. Finally, on the last day of the visit, he called the professor aside, to a place where he knew he couldn't be overheard, and said: "I have something to confess to you. Many years ago, when I was a young boy, my grandmother took me to church and had me baptized. She never told my parents, who were members of the Party, and she made me promise that I would keep the secret. I've never thought much about it. But, tell me, did something happen? Am I really baptized?"

This man's story leads to two reflections: First: Yes, something did happen; something was happening. In the midst of a society officially committed to one view of history, another very different view was being upheld, not by scholarly debate nor by philosophical disquisition, but by a liturgy that understood its purpose as grafting participants into that other history. In his baptism, that young boy had "renounced the Devil and all his works," and even though he had officially renounced Christ and all his works, he was not quite sure what it all meant. Baptism, seen not as a symbolic event, nor even as a washing away of sin, but as a grafting into a different history, kept tugging at the man. Second: Looking now at our own situation, one wonders if our liturgical practices would lead to any such reaction.

Christianity differs radically from the mystery religions that were so popular in the Mediterranean basin during the first centuries of the Christian era, and whose modern counterparts are so popular in our day. During the first two or three decades of the twentieth century, there was much research into these mystery religions, and many scholars concluded that Christianity was simply one more among many such religions. The parallels were many. Baptism, with its imagery of being washed in the blood of the Lamb, seemed very similar to the taurobolia, in which initiates of Mithra were washed in the blood of a bull; and the resurrection of Jesus was parallelled to the resurrection of Osiris after Seth dismembered him and scattered his body all over Egypt.

What all of this parallelomania missed, however, and what more recent scholarship has realized, was the one radical difference between the mysteries and Christianity. The mysteries had evolved from the various fertility cults of the area. The flooding of the Nile in Egypt, and the cycle of the seasons further north, had given rise to a number of myths explaining them. In all of these myths, just as nature dies every year only to be renewed again, so does the god die, either on a yearly basis or in a transhistorical, mythological world.

Christianity, on the other hand, had sprung out of the faith of Israel, a faith which was essentially historical in character, for although the Hebrews did have myths of creation, and explanations of a number of natural phenomena, their faith was based, not on such phenomena, but on the historical deeds of God for the redemption of Israel.

Likewise, Christianity did not speak of a God who dies and is raised every year, nor of one who dies and is raised in the mythological world of the gods, but of a God incarnate in history, who died and rose only once, at a given date. When children first learn the Apostles' Creed, they often wonder why Pontius Pilate seems to be blamed for the crucifixion in a particular way, when there were so many actors in the drama. Hopefully, later they realize that the inclusion of Pilate in the Creed is not an attempt to blame him, but an affirmation that the Creed is speaking about historical, datable facts.

The ground of baptism and eucharist is not some eternal principle, nor some recurring cycle. The ground of baptism and eucharist is the historical event, Jesus Christ. And, because they are so grounded, baptism and eucharist, every time they are celebrated, are themselves also historical events. They are *types* linking our history with the *archetype* of all history, Jesus Christ, who suffered, was crucified, dead, buried and raised again, "under Pontius Pilate."

If the use of typology lessened greatly after the rise of Constantine, it is no wonder that it is making a return at this point when the Constantinian age is ending in the West. Nor is it a wonder that typology is extensively employed in some of the younger churches that have never been part of the Constantinian arrangement.

In the present liturgical renewal, the Roman Catholic Church and many of the traditional Protestant churches have dramatically changed their liturgies for baptism and the eucharist. One can compare these new liturgies and see that they are far more parallel to each other than most are to their own church's liturgies of fifty years ago. They also have more in common with the early church than they have with the sixteenth century. The recent Lima document of the World Council of Churches—*Baptism, Eucharist and Ministry*—shows the commonalities very well. Even if such a document could have been produced fifty years ago, it would have shown nowhere near the areas of agreement across denominational and confessional lines. The change is not antiquarian, it is quite practical. The second and third century churches understood the power of liturgy—well done—to create and nurture Christian identity. Liturgy was a major means of helping people to know what it meant to be a Christian, and to live their lives out of that understanding. The surrounding culture could hardly be expected to help in that process.

In the Constantinian period, one could assume that the whole society was Christian, and that Christian identity was seldom "over-against" the culture in which it expressed itself. But in an increasingly secular society, we find ourselves in great need of these means of Christian identity-formation. This is what has made the ancient liturgies particularly relevant. When the rediscovery of ancient manuscripts and the academic study of liturgy came forth with more accurate descriptions of early forms of Christian worship, churches adapted them readily to their own contemporary situations. For instance, the renunciations in baptism, which were part of early liturgies, make sense at a time when it is clear that Christians must not only affirm what they believe, but must also reject and turn from many of the values and beliefs of the societies in which they live.

The liturgical renewal includes more than the sacraments. Even in Protestant churches that once celebrated little more than the Lord's Day, the church calendar has taken new root. The seasons of the year provide dramatic ways in which the teachings of the church can be reinforced in the home. Although such things as the secularized versions of Christmas create new problems, the celebrations still provide great opportunities for Christian nurture beyond the walls of the church. Along with the church year has come a new interest in the lectionary within churches that had little sympathy for such matters a few years ago.

It may be that the increased secularism that surrounds the churches has caused us to seek for what can create in us a common Christian identity. Even if we do not worship together most of the time, perhaps we can read the same texts and celebrate the same seasons, in an ad hoc ecumenism that may in the long run prove crucial to our growing together.

In this context, let us look again at David, in the narrative of his battle with Goliath that was mentioned above. The account of the anointing of the young David, while Saul is still king, occurs in the present lectionary late in the Lenten season. Typologically, this makes great sense. Even as David was anointed to be king while another was still ruling, so those who are to be baptized at Easter will also be anointed as the royal and priestly people of God. Those of us for whom the baptism of others at Easter is a reminder and our renewal of our baptismal vows are also reminded that we have been similarly anointed. (In this context, it is significant to note that the anointing with oil as a part of the baptismal service is being restored by many churches that would not have considered it until recently.) Just as young David took on the struggle with Goliath and was victorious, so too we who are baptized will be called upon to struggle against the powers that are raised against us. We too can be confident of some surprising victories. Even as the victory brought David the jealousy and enmity of Saul who was still king, we too can anticipate the animosity and antagonism of the powers of this world that do still rule. In all of this, David pre-figures and we who are now baptized experience in our own lives, the archetype—Jesus who is Christ—the anointed one, who in this Lenten season is approaching the apex of the enmity he has aroused because of his victories. To be baptized is to be added to this line, this history. It is an event. It teaches us not only something about David; not only something about Jesus; it also teaches us about ourselves— who we are because we are baptized.

Typological forms are not only in the words that we preach. They abound in the liturgy.[3] They are not the creation of the later church, but are found in Scripture itself. The manna in the wilderness is a type of the Bread from heaven that is Jesus. The words of the Gospel of John are clear: "I am the bread of life. Your ancestors ate the manna in the wilderness, and they died. . . . I am the living bread that came down from heaven. . . . and the bread that I will give for the life of the world is my flesh" (John 6:48, 51). Or the words of Paul: "Our ancestors were all under the cloud, and all passed through the sea, and all were baptized into Moses in the cloud and in the sea, and all ate the same spiritual food, and all drank the same spiritual drink. For they drank from the spiritual rock that followed them, and the rock was Christ" (I Cor. 10:1-4). The manna in the wilderness was an act of God for the nourishment and salvation of the people, a gracious and loving act for a people newly set free from bondage, now entered into a covenant, and still on their way to a future land. It was an event at a specific time in the life of the people. The Eucharist is a new manna for the covenant people newly set free from the bondage to sin and death, now on their way to the future Reign of God. We need food for the journey. There are clear parallels or analogies between these two instances of feeding. But in the light of the work of Christ, the manna in the wilderness is an event that points to the greater event to come.

Our communion services are events that point back to the work of Christ. The Cross and the Resurrection are the *archetype* of both that which comes before and that which comes after. But all are events. They take place at a specific moment in history. They are datable, witnessable events, even if all who see them do not understand the meaning or the significance. Some at the cross did not understand. In this way, types are more than symbols. They do more than point to something else. They are in their own right events that bring into the present the power and significance of the archetype upon which they are based. They are repetitions in a way, but with their own locus in a particular history, so that they are never simple duplications of the archetype. The Eucharist is not the Cross, but it is an event in which the power of the Cross is brought to us. Nor are eucharistic services identical to one another, for they occur in different historical moments.

The sacraments are clearly types. But they are not the only ones. In a sense the whole church year has a typological character, helping us in our own time to recapture and enter into the significant events of redemption in the life and work of Jesus. Advent and Christmas services, Lent, Easter, Pentecost, and all of the others, are specific moments in our contemporary life as the people of God when we can be renewed as who we are. They are not repetitions. Christ is not born every winter, nor does he die and rise again in the spring. His birth, death and resurrection were indeed once and for all. But they are archetypes of events that still occur, allowing our participation in them, even as there were parallel events before his coming that were based on that advent and prepared the people for it.

The Pulpit As a Connecting Point

Rarely will the simple reading of a passage of Scripture in the midst of worship cause that worship to become a new event, a new occasion of the biblical pattern. Almost always the connection must be made, and that connection is the task of preaching. The Reformation made this explicit in the linking of Word and Sacrament. But often we have understood this connection in a legalistic fashion: that there must be preaching when the Eucharist is celebrated, though we are not always clear as to why. We may also assume there ought to be preaching when baptism is celebrated, though for many Protestant churches, there is no assumption that the sermon should have anything at all to do with baptism. It is somehow sufficient to have the two items in the same service. What the connection is, however, is totally unclear. In fact, where infant baptism is the usual form, the baptism may well take place early in the service, so that the infant won't be cranky, and then the rest of the worship goes on as though there had been no baptism. The requirement has been met, but the rationale is missing.

In the case of the Eucharist, usually there is a sense that the sacrament should follow the sermon because some specific connection is expected. Some preachers and congregations oppose frequent communion for fear sermons on the topic of communion would become highly repetitious. The Reformation period saw a variety of understandings of the relationship of sermon and sacrament, and it was a central issue for the Protestants. For some, the emphasis was on the necessity of making clear to the congregation what was—and was not—believed about the Lord's Supper and baptism. That led to a highly didactic approach. That, indeed, could become repetitious. For others, there was a more intimate association—that somehow the Word preached was incomplete without the Sacrament received, since the sacrament brought to us what the Word promised. Such an understanding would hardly lead to repetitious sermons, since the specific passage of Scripture for any particular sermon would lead to a varied nuancing of the sacrament itself. This view, however, lost out in the centuries following the Reformation. The legalistic and didactic perceptions remained.

We recommend a revival of liturgical preaching. However, before we go much further, it is necessary to clarify what we mean by such "liturgical preaching." It is not simply preaching about the liturgy. Indeed, the very phrase "liturgical preaching" may cause some revulsion among many of us, for we have heard too much liturgical preaching that is little more than ecclesiastical navel-gazing, in which we extol the beauty of the liturgical tradition, with little relevance for life in today's world.

On Christmas Eve 1989 we attended a beautiful service, graced with choral music from different periods in the history of the church, music rejoicing in the presence of God with us. Then came the sermon. It was a well-written piece. It was not particularly profound. But that was not its greatest fault. What was missing, particularly in a service celebrating the incarnation, was any reference to the world to which God has come. The United States had invaded Panama; people were killing each other in Romania; there was talk of a new world being born in Eastern Europe; repression was the order of the day in the Holy Land; and we spoke of the meaning of Christmas with no reference to any of those events.

That was the first thing missing in that service. But then, there was something else that was amis, for after the sermon—and with no other explanation or connecting word, we all opened our books while the minister read: "All ye who do truly and earnestly repent of your sins." And we had communion. The problem is not that we had communion at a Christmas service. That would have been very good indeed. The problem was that we celebrated communion with no connection to the sermon, to the rest of the liturgy, or to the world around us.

111

In that service the liturgy was governed by a non-historical, non-typological perspective. The meaning of Christmas had little or nothing to do with the world to which Jesus has come, and the eucharist was a self-contained reality somehow expressing eternal truths, which therefore can be celebrated anywhere and anytime, without necessary reference to the time or place of the celebration.

The best liturgical preaching is grounded on an understanding of liturgy as event—as event significant and signified. The event is signified—is made a sign—by Christ, who has given the liturgy its character as a sign both of *who he is* and *who we are* in relationship to him. "Take, eat, this is my body which is for you." Those words say something about the event; but they also say something both about the speaker and about those who are to receive this bread. All of this is signified in that liturgical event. And, precisely because all of this is signified, the event is significant. The event both makes us who we are and shows us who we are.

Preaching within the community of faith is in some sense always a sacramental event. Whether or not a sacrament is being celebrated, it is a gathering of the baptized people. Our problem is that we are not always clear to whom we are preaching, and that affects the possible use of a typological form.

In the United States, coming out of the history of the great evangelical revivals of the eighteenth and nineteenth centuries, we have lost much of the distinction that earlier centuries had concerning preaching within the community of faith and preaching to the unconverted. Revivals today assume that those to whom preaching was addressed had once been faithful, but had somehow lapsed and were in need of being urged to return. But this means that there are three groups to which preaching might conceivably be addressed: those who are strangers to the faith—missionary preaching; those who once were faithful but have lapsed from that state—revival preaching; and those who are the faithful. In North American society, what we came to call "evangelistic preaching" was addressed to the second of those groups—those who understood the faith but had lapsed from it. However, it gradually became the model for all preaching, within and outside the church.

The early church assumed that those gathered for preaching were the faithful. Others might be there—especially catechumens who were still to be baptized and penitents who were temporarily excommunicated—and they were there to hear the words addressed to the faithful. Of course there was missionary preaching—but that was done outside of the church. We have mixed preaching to those outside of the church and preaching to the faithful in such a fashion that the mission always seems to be to the faithful. We have lost much of the ability to speak clearly to those outside the church, and that should cause us grave concern. But our point here is that an evangelistic form of preaching assumes that those within the church have to begin again every Sunday, and that also has grave consequences for our preaching. With such an assumption there can be little growth and development of faith for believers. The fact that the preaching is addressed to a baptized congregation should make a difference in the biblical interpretation and the preaching. Scripture is a word already addressed to God's People—even the history of a dialogue between God and God's People. The congregation is not there to choose whether to be part of this people—they already are. Baptism is the sign of that inclusion. Therefore the word is for them. The preacher needs to make clear the connection of that ancient word to this present People of God. Typology assumes the continuity of the People of God, and therefore the word to that ancient people can readily be applied to the congregation now gathered.

The preaching event does not occur in a vacuum. It is an historical event. That means that it is somehow linked, not only to a long series of past events, but also to other contemporary events. The celebration of Christmas in that year of 1989, the proclamation of God with us, was linked to events in Panama and in Romania, and to break that link is to diminish its significance. The gathering at the Lord's table on that Christmas must have had something to do both with the meaning of Christmas and with the fact that that very night millions of people throughout the world did not have enough to eat.

In contrast to what happened on that Christmas Eve service, true liturgical preaching is grounded in the historical and typological perspective. Jesus Christ is the archetype through which we must read all of Scripture, all the liturgy, and all of history, including our own. Ideally, what occurs in the liturgical celebration is that we are grafted into and nourished by a history whose key and goal is Jesus Christ, so that the liturgical event itself is a type of Christ, and the preaching binds together Scripture, life and liturgical event.

Preaching is not just the act of the preacher. It is also the act of a community that recognizes its faith in the words of the preacher. In some of our churches we may not say "preach on, brother"; but real preaching takes place only when the congregation does say this, if not in words, at least in spirit. Preaching takes place when the community recognizes in the words of the preacher, not only its faith, but also its situation as it relates to the historic faith—in other words, as it recognizes itself within the typology of God's *oikonomía*.

There may be some specific reasons why typological preaching has been relatively rare in our society. Several years ago Catherine was involved in a preaching course at the seminary in which there was a requirement that students prepare a sermon on the topic of atonement. Each class member had to choose a biblical text and then prepare a sermon that dealt with

113

atonement, but being faithful to that specific text. One of the students choose Isaiah 53—the great Suffering Servant passage. Obviously, this is an excellent text for this purpose. But the student went straight from Isaiah 53 to the Cross of Jesus. When asked what the passage had meant to those in Israel who had heard it originally, the student's response was that it could have meant nothing. It could not have referred to Israel, or to anyone in particular in Israel, for then it could not have meant Jesus. For this student, clearly the mode of interpretation was prophecy-fulfillment. Here was a prophecy: to whom did it refer? It either referred to Jesus or to someone else. If faith held that it meant Jesus, then obviously it could not have meant anyone else. To introduce typology as a possibility meant that one could deal with the passage in terms of what it meant to the people of God to whom it was first addressed; then how it can be seen fully expressed in the life, death, and resurrection of Jesus; and finally, how it relates to us in our setting. I Peter does this very clearly, using the model of Isaiah 53 as lived out by Jesus, as the guide for Christian slaves and wives who may be unjustly treated in their non-Christian households, and whose only alternative may have been abandoning the faith.

A certain comfort results from the prophecy-fulfillment model. We can start and stop with the work of Christ. His was the cross. Our task is to believe in what he did. In no sense are we called upon to take up our cross, for that would take away from the work of Christ. Typology removes that comfort totally. It assumes the repetition in our lives of the pattern that is fully exemplified in the work of Jesus. Without such an understanding it is difficult to know how one would deal with passages such as Colossians 1:24, where the apostle writes: "Now I rejoice in my sufferings for your sake, and in my flesh I complete what is lacking in Christ's afflictions for the sake of his body, that is, the church."

The added demand on us is one reason why typology disappeared in its full form after the fourth century. Christianity, now the official religion of the Roman Empire, was increasingly equated with expected, decent behavior, but hardly with the demands that put a Christian over against the general society. If you wanted a more rigorous class of Christianity you could join the monastic forms that began to flourish at this time. But one would hardly anticipate a cross in a Christian Empire. For this reason, the repetition in our lives of the type seen fully in Christ was not something to be expected.

What was lost was not only the repetition of the difficult parts of the Gospel—the rejection, the opposition, the suffering, the dying with Christ, the Cross. Equally lost were the positive dimensions—the new birth, the new life, the victory, the resurrection, the Reign of God. Those were put off until the life after death. If we are not in a position to make the parallels on the difficult side, we are also not in a position to make the joyful parallels.

For typology, preaching has the task of making clear the relationship between the work of Christ and our lives, not losing sight of the truth that salvation hinges upon his work alone. What occurs in our lives that repeats the pattern of his is totally derivative of his work, and in fact, could be called his work in us, the church, the present manifestation in the world of the Body of Christ.

Yet, this is not to say that typology is a panacea for biblical interpretation. Typology does indeed lend itself to abuse and to misuse. We have already mentioned Eusebius of Caesarea. Eusebius wished to show that with Constantine God's purposes had come to fruition, and he therefore employed typology to declare that Constantine was the new Moses whom God has raised to lead God's people. One may well understand his reasons, and even empathize with them. The church had just come out of the most terrible of persecutions. Suddenly, in a most unexpected fashion, Christians, until recently considered the scum of society, now enjoyed a new status. And so, from the point of view of Eusebius, Constantine was the new Moses:

> Ancient history relates that a cruel race of tyrants oppressed the Hebrew nation; and that God, who graciously regarded them in their affliction, provided that the prophet Moses, who was then an infant, should be brought up in the very palaces and bosoms of the oppressors, and instructed in all the wisdom they possessed. And when in the course of time he had arrived at manhood, and the time was come for Divine justice to avenge the wrongs of the afflicted people, then the prophet of God, in obedience to the will of a more powerful Lord, forsook the royal household, and, estranging himself in word and deed from the tyrants by whom he had been brought up, openly acknowledged his true brethren and kinsfolk. Then God, exalting him to be the leader of the whole nation, delivered the Hebrews from the bondage of their enemies, and inflicted Divine vengeance through his means on the tyrant race. This ancient story, though rejected by most as fabulous, has reached the ears of all. But now the same God has given to us to be eye-witnesses of miracles more wonderful than fables, and, from their recent appearance, more authentic than any report. For the tyrants of our day have ventured to war against the Supreme God, and has sorely afflicted His Church. And in the midst of these, Constantine, who was shortly to become their destroyer, but at that time of tender age, and blooming with the down of early youth, dwelt, as that other servant of God had done.[4]

One can empathize with Eusebius' reasons. Yet, this was the beginning of a process of sacralization of the state that would prove costly to both the state and the church. Therefore, not all typology is to be commended.

What is wrong with Eusebius' typology? What lessons can we learn from it? First of all, by making Constantine the goal of history, it destroys the very foundation of Christian typology, which is the finality of Jesus Christ. He is the archetype of which Moses is the type. There can be no finality other than

Jesus himself, nor can there be a conclusion to the types in our history, derivative of his work, until the end of history itself in Christ's reign.

Secondly, Eusebius's typology about Constantine indicates the constant need for perspectives beyond the limited circles in which we move. There were many Christians at the time who felt the brunt of Constantine's power, and might not have agreed with this typology. Christians in the West were among them, but many monastics in the East also distrusted such a typology.

The Pilgrims who came to New England could quite understandably use the typology of the Exodus as they left religious persecution in England and came to the New World. Clearly, this new world was to them the Promised Land. But in their use of this typology, their descendants soon forgot that the fullness of such a typology ultimately centers in the Cross. Within our national consciousness, being the Promised Land took on secular, national forms, and all those who could be considered "Canaanites" could be eliminated. No Cross, no redemptive suffering could be expected for this Chosen People. The dangers of the misuse of typology can be greatly diminished if the centrality of the Cross is remembered. Then the self-serving typologies that lead to privilege can be lessened.

The first of the great leaders of the church in the generation immediately after Constantine was Athanasius. Still a young boy at the time when persecutions ceased, Athanasius did not have opportunity to experience the positive side of the contrast between the times before and after the conversion of Constantine. Perhaps for that reason he was freer than an older man like Eusebius of Caesarea to see the dangers in the new situation. His relations with imperial authority were by no means easy or entirely happy.

In 358, Athanasius wrote and published anonymously a blistering attack on Constantius, one of Constantine's sons. There he calls Constantius "patron of impiety and Emperor of heresy," "this modern Ahab, this second Belshazzar," the "enemy of Christ, leader of impiety, and as it were antichrist himself." He goes on to question the very authority of the Emperor which Eusebius had so extolled:

> When was such a thing heard of before from the beginning of the world? When did a judgment of the Church receive its validity from the Emperor? or rather when was his decree ever recognized by the Church? There have been many councils held heretofore; and many judgments passed by the Church; but the Fathers never sought the consent of the Emperor thereto, nor did the Emperor busy himself with the affairs of the Church.[5]

What led Athanasius to this conclusion, so drastically different from that of Eusebius, was first of all his own experience of exile and persecution, but also his contact with the monastics and his solidarity with the poor, for whom Constantius and his party showed little regard. Indeed, when Athanasius found it necessary to disappear, he was hidden by the monks. Athanasius claimed that one of the most disgraceful things that the Arians had done was to join the powerful in their disregard for the poor, the widows and the orphans. He tells the story of the collaboration in Alexandria between Duke Sebastian, the representative of the Emperor, and the Arians. Among other incidents, he declares that when the Duke gave the churches to the Arians, the latter expelled the poor and the widows who used to receive sustenance from the church. The orthodox clergy in charge of these services assigned places where these people in need could meet in order to receive their ministrations. The Arians retaliated by beating the widows and accusing their benefactors before the authorities, knowing that the Emperor was on their side.

Clearly, the opinion of Eusebius was not the only one, nor did he speak for the entire church. His typology was done without the input of other voices.

No method of biblical interpretation can guard against limited vision and self-serving interpretations. Only other parts of the Christian community can do that—those who are not part of our social class, our national identity, our political persuasion, and yet who are equally devout Christians. The use of typology does not rule out biases from such social and economic sources. Some of the most fruitful discussions among Christians, however, may be on the basis of where in Scripture we find the parallels to our contemporary situation. By comparing these, by discussing the alternative typologies that can be used, we may find common ground that we had not expected. Scripture has the capacity to challenge our perspectives with its own. Other Christians, who are in different situations, can help that happen.

What we are advocating in a return to early typology as a basis for preaching is the restoration of the unity of Scripture, liturgy, and preaching, all bound up in the fiber of life. Together they have a power that is severely weakened when they are separated. What happens when they are placed together is no longer that we interpret Scripture, or that we explain the meaning of the sacrament. What happens is rather that Scripture interprets us, that the sacrament illumines life, and that life illumines both Scripture and the sacrament. Thus a hermeneutical circulation is established in which our place in history, the liturgical celebration and the text of Scripture interpret each other.

But an example is worth much more than a thousand theories. In the following excerpt from a now famous sermon, note the connection between the liturgical event which was about to be celebrated, the historical setting, and the life of the congregation and the preacher. The sermon itself was preached on March 24, 1980, in a relatively small hospital chapel in San Salvador. The texts are I Corinthians 15, and the saying of Jesus, "whoever would save his life will lose it, and whoever loses his life for my sake will find it" (Matt. 16:25). The preacher is Msgr. Oscar Arnulfo Romero. The occasion is a memorial eucharist. A month earlier, there had already been an attempt to blow up the cathedral while Romero was celebrating communion. What follows is only a selection of a few relevant passages that illustrate the character of true liturgical, typological preaching. The interweaving of text, occasion, historical setting, and the life of the preacher himself is dramatic:[6]

> I believe, my brothers and sisters, that this afternoon you should not only pray for the eternal rest of our beloved who is deceased; but you should also take up this message that must be intensively lived today by every Christian. Many people surprise us by claiming that Christianity has nothing to do with these things. [The struggles of the Salvadoran people for justice and liberation.] But exactly the opposite is true.
>
> You have just heard the words from the Gospel of Christ, that we must not love ourselves so much that we refrain from taking the risks of life that history today requires of us; and you have heard that those who seek to avoid danger will lose their lives. On the other hand, those who give themselves up in service to others for love of Christ, they will live; just as the grain of wheat that seems to die, but does not. If it does not die, it will remain alone. There is a harvest because it dies, because it allows itself to be sacrificed in the soil, to be undone, and by being undone it produces the harvest. . . .
>
> I ask all of you, my dear brothers and sisters, that we look upon these things of our historical moment with this same hope, with this same spirit of self-giving, of sacrifice, and that we each do what we can. . . .
>
> This Holy Mass, this Eucharist, is precisely that, an act of faith. It is by faith that we know that this host of wheat becomes the body of Christ which was offered for the redemption of the world, and that in that chalice the wine becomes the blood which was the price for our salvation. May this broken body and this blood shed for humankind nourish us, so that we too may give up our bodies and our blood to suffering and to pain, like Christ; not for ourselves, but in order to bring forth visions of justice and of peace for our people. Let us therefore come closely together in faith and in hope as we pray both for Doña Sarita and for ourselves.
>
> (At that moment, a shot was fired.)

In this dramatic event, Scripture, liturgy, and preaching are inseparably linked. They are not only related to an historical moment, but in themselves they create such a moment—an event in which Scripture was fully interpreted; the liturgy was fully lived out, and the preaching fully united them. The resultant martyrdom may help to explain why such preaching is infrequent.

Does all such preaching lead to dying? Perhaps there is a connection between being ready to see and live out the full implications of the Gospel and an excellent, true use of typology. But Romero's life before this had shown the freedom, the power, and the victory that the Gospel brings. Like David, he had overcome some Goliaths. Like Saul, the evil of the old order sought to kill him, and finally did, though it could end neither his true life nor its influence.

A new vision of preaching is required. Preaching is not an event in itself—the sermon— but is rather the midwife of an event—the liturgy, the total act of worship. The sermon points to the current historical setting in which the congregation lives its daily life and in which this liturgy is set, with its pain and injustice; with its yearnings and hopes. It points to the ancient word in which God spoke to the People of God in their historical setting. The sermon shows the parallels and the differences, preparing for the Word to become present. The liturgy is the vehicle for this presence: in the recognition of our baptism, in the celebration of the eucharist, in the seasons of the year, in the prayers of the people, or by other aspects of worship. The sermon is not an end in itself, nor is its effect necessarily directly upon the worshippers. Its power and fruitfulness may only be seen in the whole event of that gathering for worship.

Often we preach as though the purpose of worship were to give directions for what Christians should do when they leave. Obviously, there is a truth in that. But if something does not happen in worship, little will happen beyond it. The sermon has the power to cause worship—the liturgy—to be a new event, a renewal of the Exodus, an occasion of our dying, a moment in which we prodigals are greeted by the Father and given a banquet.

The liturgy, well done, brings to our experience the ancient story of God's People by means of the sermon, and tells us who we are. It is as God's People that we leave the service. In worship, we are called back and re-enact the central themes of that history, nuanced each time by our historical setting and by different portions of the whole spectrum of the biblical witness.

The task of the sermon is to let the Word speak through the worship so that the People of God, the Body of Christ, is nurtured, strengthened, renewed, rehearsed in who they are.

If it is not the People of God who leave the sanctuary, there is little hope they will transform the world. The early church knew how to put together as one event the Scripture, the sermon, and the liturgy, in order to form such a People. It is a skill and a vision we must relearn.

Notes

Preface

1. Catherine Gunsalus González, "The Use of the Bible in Hymns, Liturgy, and Education," in *The New Interpreter's Bible*, vol 1 (Nashville: Abingdon, 1994).

2. Justo L. González, "How the Bible Has Been Interpreted in Christian Tradition," *The New Interpreter's Bible*, vol. 1 (Nashville: Abingdon, 1994).

3. Justo L. González, *Faith and Wealth: A History of Early Christian Ideas on the Origin, Significance, and Use of Money* (San Francisco: Harper & Row, 1990).

4. Justo L, González, *Out of Every Tribe and Nation: Christian Theology at the Ethnic Roundtable* (Nashville: Abingdon, 1992).

Chapter I: A New Way of Doing Theology

1. The classical and seminal study on this subject is Albert Memmi's *The Colonizer and the Colonized* (Boston: Beacon, 1965).

2. *Church History*, 3.25.

3. Palladius says that, according to a local bishop, there were in the region of Oxyrhynchus twenty thousand nuns and ten thousand monks. He also says that there were more monastic houses than private residences. *Hist. lausiaca*, 5. Cf. *idem*, 58.

4. One of the best books on the subject, published precisely at the time of the Quincentennial, is Luis N. Rivera-Pagán's *A Violent Evangelism: The Political and Religious Conquest of the Americas* (Louisville: Westminster / John Knox, 1992).

5. Letty M. Russell, *Human Liberation in a Feminist Perspective: A Theology* (Philadelphia: Westminster, 1974), p. 58.

6. James H. Cone, *God of the Oppressed* (New York: Seabury, 1975), pp. 30-31.

7. This may be seen, for instance, in the wide range of subjects discussed by Juan Luis Segundo in *A Theology for Artisans of a New Humanity* (Maryknoll, N.Y.: Orbis Books, 1973). The titles of the five volumes make this clear: *The Community Called Church, Grace and the Human Condition, Our Idea of God, The Sacraments Today,* and *Evolution and Guilt.* In a similar vein, see Justo L. González, *Mañana: Christian Theology from a Hispanic Perspective* (Nashville: Abingdon, 1990), which includes chapters on the doctrine of God, the Trinity, creation, Christology, anthropology, etc.

8. "El sujeto histórico de la teología de la liberación," in *Taller de teología, II: Praxis cristiana y producción teológica en América Latina* (México: Comunidad Teológica de México, 1972), p. 9.

9. For a more thorough exploration of these three perspectives throughout Christian history, and their implications both in theological and in socio-political terms, see Justo L. González, *Christian Thought Revisited: Three Types of Theology* (Nashville: Abingdon, 1989).

10. *A Black Theology of Liberation* (Philadelphia: J.B. Lippincott, 1970), p. 93.

11. *Human Liberation*, p. 53.

12. Rosemary Reuther, *Liberation Theology: Human Hope Confronts Christian History and American Power* (New York: Paulist Press, 1972), p. 3.

13. *A Theology of Liberation: History, Politics, and Salvation* (Maryknoll, N.Y.: Orbis Books, 1973), p. 10.

14. *Black Theology*, pp. 131-32.

15. In Shaull and Gutiérrez, *Liberation and Change* (Atlanta: John Knox Press, 1977), pp. 100-101.

Chapter II: Difficulties In Hearing the Text

1. *The Liberation of Theology* (Maryknoll, N.Y.: Orbis Books, 1976), p. 9.

2. V. Elizondo, *Galilean Journey: The Mexican-American Promise* (Maryknoll, N.Y.: Orbis, 1983); O.E. Costas, "Evangelism from the Periphery: A Galilean Model," *Apuntes* 2 (1982), pp. 51-59; "Evangelism from the Periphery: The Universality of Galilee," *Apuntes* 2 (1982), pp. 75-84.

3. William L. Wonderly, *Bible Translations for Popular Use* (New York: United Bible Societies, 1968), p. 51.

4. See the articles *adelphos* and *pater* in William F. Arndt and F. Wilbur Gingrich, *A Greek-English Lexicon of the New Testament* (Chicago: University of Chicago Press, 1957).

5. Consultation on Common Texts, *The Revised Common Lectionary* (Nashville: Abingdon, 1992).

6. Walter Brueggemann, *Texts under Negotiation: The Bible and Postmodern Imagination* (Minneapolis: Fortress, 1993), p. 58.

7. Edited by C.A. Newsom and S.H. Ringe (London: SPCK, 1992).

8. Published in Miami by Editorial Caribe, 1989.

Chapter III: The Neglected Interpreters

1. *Ep. ad Smyrnaeos*, 6.2 (BAC 65:492). This quotation as well as most of those that follow, and hundreds of others, may be found in Juan Leuridá, ed., *Justicia y explotatión en la tradición cristiana antigua* (Lima: Centro de Estudios y Publicaciones, 1973) and in the more extensive collection by R. Sierra Bravo, *Doctrina social y económica de los padres de la iglesia* (Madrid: Compañía Bibliográfica Española, 1967).

2. *Simil.*, 10.4.2-3 (BAC 65:1091).

3. *De Nabuthe Jezraelita*, 1.1 (PL 14:767).

4. *De officiis ministrorum*, 1.28.132 (PL 16.62).

5. *De Nab. Jez.*, 1.11 (PL 14:783).

6. *Expositio Evangelii secundum Lucam*, 7.124 (PL 15:1731).

7. *De Nab. Jez.*, 1.3 (PL 14:769).

8. *Ibid.*, 1.1 (PL 14:767).

9. *Homilia in illud Lucam, Destruam . . .*, 7 (PG 31:277).

10. *Homilia de Lazaro*, 2.6 (PG 48:992).

11. *Homilia in Psalmum xiv* (PG 29:273).

12. *Homilia in divites*, 5 (PG 31:293).

13. *Epistola cxx* (PL 22:984).

14. *De justitia*, 5 (PL 11:286).

15. *Enarratio in Psalmum cxxxi* (PL 37:1718).

16. *Divinarum Institutionum libri septem*, 5.5 (PL 6:565).

17. *Comment. in Lucam* v.x (PG 72:816).

18. *Regulae Pastoralis liber*, 3.21 (PL 77:87).

19. *In Ep. I ad Thimoteum*, 4.12.3 (PG 62:562).

20. *Ibid.*, 4.12.4 (PG 62:563).

21. *Homilia de Lazaro*, 6.8 (PG 48:1039).

22. *In Mattaeum homilia lxxvii* (PG 58:708).

23. *In Joannem homilia lxv* 3 (PG 59:364).

24. *In Psalmum xlviii*, 3 (PG 55:517).

25. *De Poenitentia*, 7.7 (PG 49:335).

26. See, for instance, the startling words of John Wesley quoted by Ronald J. Sider, *Rich Christians in an Age of Hunger* (Downers Grove, Ill.: Intervarsity Press, 1977), pp. 172-73. See also, for a fuller account of Wesley's views on the matter, T. W. Jennings, Jr., *Good News to the Poor: John Wesley's Evangelical Economics* (Nashville: Abingdon, 1990).

27. *In Ecclesiasten Salomonis homilia* iv (PG 44:665).

28. *On the Dress of Virgins*, 22 (ANF 5:436).

29. *Adv. haer.*, V.33 (*ANF*, I:563).

30. Some examples are: Elsa Tamez, ed., *Through Her Eyes: Women's Theology from Latin America* (Maryknoll, N.Y.: Orbis, 1989); Elsa Tamez, *The Sacandalous Message of James* (New York: Crossroads, 1990); Kwok Pui-Lan, *Chinese Women and Christianity, 1860-1927* (Atlanta: Scholars Press, 1992).

31. Ernesto Cardenal, *The Gospel in Solentiname*, 4 vols. (Maryknoll, N.Y.: Orbis Books, 1976-1982). The examples used here come from vol. I.

32. Ibid., pp. 15-16.

33. Ibid., p. 18.

34. Ibid., p. 62.

35. Ibid., pp. 154, 152.

36. Letty M. Russell, ed., *The Liberating Word: A Guide to Nonsexist Interpretation of the Bible* (Philadelphia: Westminster Press, 1976), p. 62.

37. Ibid., p. 65.

38. Rachel Conrad Wahlberg, *Jesus According to a Woman* (New York: Paulist Press, 1975), p. 44.

39. Ibid., p. 65.

40. Gerald H. Anderson and Thomas F. Stransky, eds., *Mission Trends No. 3: Third World Theologies* (New York: Paulist Press, 1976), pp. 152-54.

41. Kim Yong Bok, ed., *Minjung Theology* (Singapore: The Christian Conference of Asia, 1981); Kim Yong Bok, *Messiah and Minjung: Christ's Solidarity with the People for New Life* (Hong Kong: The Christian Conference of Asia, 1992); Mun Hui-Sok, *A Korean Minjung Theology: An Old Testament Perspective* (Maryknoll, N.Y.: Orbis, 1985); Lee Sang Hyun, ed., *Essays on Korean Heritage and Christianity* (Princeton Junction, N.J.: Association of Korean Christian Scholars of North America, 1984).

42. *The Wounded Heart of God: The Asian Concept of Han and the Christian Doctrine of Sin* (Nashville: Abingdon, 1993), p. 103.

43. Ibid., pp. 112-114.

NOTES

Chapter IV: Some Pointers On Biblical Interpretation

1. Herbert Marshall McLuhan, *Understanding Media: The Extension of Man* (New York: McGraw-Hill, 1964).
2. *Commentary on Joshua* (Grand Rapids: Eerdmans, 1949), p. 46.
3. See J. Rius-Camps, *El camino de Pablo a la misión de los paganos* (Madrid: Cristiandad, 1984), p. 27; P. Gächter, *Petrus und seine Zeit* (Innsbruck: Tyrolia-Verlag, 1958), pp. 105-154.
4. Tertullian, *De idol.*, 15.
5. *Freedom Made Flesh: The Mission of Christ and His Church* (Maryknoll, N.Y.: Orbis Books, 1976), p. 80.
6. On the customs and laws regarding marriage, the authority of the *pater familias*, and slavery, see the articles "Marriage," "Manus," "Familia," "Emancipation," "Freedmen," "Mancipium," "Coemptio," and "Slaves" in Oskar Seyffert, *Dictionary of Classical Antiquities*, edition revised by H. Nettleship and J. E. Sandys (New York: Meridian Library, 1956). For less detail, see Lionel Casson, *Daily Life in Ancient Rome* (New York: McGraw-Hill, 1975).
7. *Texts Under Negotiation*, pp. 59-60.
8. We have discussed this matter more fully in a sermon and commentary in A. Van Seters, ed., *Preaching as a Social Act: Theology and Practice* (Nashville: Abingdon, 1988), pp. 41-54.

Chapter V: Making Connections

1. This is not to say that all members of the early church were poor. Wayne A. Meeks has studied the social status of those members mentioned by name in the Pauline epistles, and has come to the conclusion that "the extreme top and bottom of the Greco-Roman social scale are missing from the picture. . . . There may have been members of the Pauline communities who lived at the subsistence level, but we hear nothing of them." The one fact that is true is that even "the most active and prominent members of Paul's circle (including Paul himself) are people of high status inconsistency." *The First Urban Christians: The Social World of the Apostle Paul* (New Haven: Yale University Press, 1983), p. 73.
2. In Eusebius' time, Revelation was generally accepted as part of the New Testament. Eusebius, however, quoted extensively from Dionysius of Alexandria, who had expressed reservations about this particular book, and on that basis raised doubts about the inclusion of the book in the canon. *Church History* 7. 25. Cf. 3. 24-25.
3. An excellent resource on the liturgical use of biblical types is Jean Daniélou, *The Bible and the Liturgy* (Notre Dame, Ind.: University of Notre Dame Press, 1956).
4. *Vita Const.* 1.12 (*NPNF*, 1:485).
5. *Hist. arianorum ad monachos* 52 (*NPNF*, 2nd. ser., 4:289).
6. Translated from a tape recording.